THINK LIKE A LAWYER

THINK LIKE A LAWYER

The Art of Argument For Law Students

Gary Fidel
and
Linda Cantoni

Library of Congress Number: 2004094844
ISBN : Hardcover 1-4134-6148-4
Softcover 1-4134-6147-6

This book was printed in the United States of America.

ThinkLikeALawyer.com, LLC New York City

To order additional copies of this book, contact:
Xlibris Corporation
1-888-795-4274
www.Xlibris.com
Orders@Xlibris.com
24848

Fidel: For Loretta

Cantoni: To Alex

CONTENTS

INTRODUCTION 13

PART ONE: THE BASICS

RULE ONE
Argument Is a Craft 19

RULE TWO
The Goal of Argument Is to Persuade 21

RULE THREE
The Simple Declarative Sentence Is Your Best Weapon 22

RULE FOUR
The More Complicated the Argument, The Simpler Your Presentation Should Be 24

RULE FIVE
Before You Write or State Your Argument, You Must Be Sure What It Is 25

RULE SIX
Stream of Consciousness Has No Place in Your Argument 26

RULE SEVEN
An Argument May Be Legal, Factual, or Both 28

RULE EIGHT
Contentions Are the Building Blocks of an Argument 32

RULE NINE
A Contention Is a Positive Statement That Can Be Made in One Sentence 34

RULE TEN
Your Contentions Must Prove Your Main Argument 36

RULE ELEVEN
Arrange Your Contentions In Descending Order of Importance 38

RULE TWELVE
A Contention Should Be The Topic Sentence of Every Paragraph 40

RULE THIRTEEN
The Body of Each Paragraph Should Prove The Truth of Its Topic Sentence Contention 43

RULE FOURTEEN
The Last Sentence of Each Paragraph Should Nail the Proof into the Reader's Mind 45

RULE FIFTEEN
The Last Sentence of Each Paragraph Should Lead into the Next Topic Sentence Contention 47

PART TWO: THE COMPLEX ARGUMENT

RULE SIXTEEN
The Point Is the Basic Organizing Tool Of Your Brief 51

RULE SEVENTEEN
Set Up Your Points 54

RULE EIGHTEEN
The Intro Paragraph Frames the Issue 56

RULE NINETEEN
The Procedural Contention Should Stand Alone 59

RULE TWENTY
Your Legal Principles Must Be Stated Before Your Facts 63

RULE TWENTY-ONE
Be Objective in Stating Your Legal Basis 65

RULE TWENTY-TWO
Use Block Quotes Sparingly 66

RULE TWENTY-THREE
Translate Legalese into Simple English 71

RULE TWENTY-FOUR
Conclude Your Law Paragraph with a Contention 73

RULE TWENTY-FIVE
Link the Facts to Your Main Argument 75

RULE TWENTY-SIX
Legal References Should Be in Plain English 78

RULE TWENTY-SEVEN
Avoid the Straw Man 80

RULE TWENTY-EIGHT
Attack Your Opponent's Legal Principles 82

RULE TWENTY-NINE
Attack Your Opponent's Facts ... 83

RULE THIRTY
Avoid the Defensive ... 85

RULE THIRTY-ONE
End Your Point with a Conclusion Paragraph ... 86

RULE THIRTY-TWO
An Argument Is a Unified Entity ... 88

PART THREE: WRITING A STATEMENT OF FACTS

RULE ONE
Tell a Story ... 91

RULE TWO
Be Accurate and Objective ... 94

RULE THREE
Don't Editorialize the Facts ... 95

RULE FOUR
Banish the Word "Testify" From Your Account ... 96

RULE FIVE
Banish the Passive Voice ... 97

RULE SIX
Rely on Bare Facts ... 99

RULE SEVEN
Close the Gaps ... 100

RULE EIGHT
Don't Run from Inconsistencies 101

RULE NINE
Put Subheadings in Their Place 102

RULE TEN
Dialogue Adds Realism 103

RULE ELEVEN
If You Have a Source, Cite It 104

RULE TWELVE
Complex Facts Require Simple Narratives 105

RULE THIRTEEN
Name Names in Your Narrative 106

RULE FOURTEEN
Your Narrative Should Be Riveting but Reliable 107

CONCLUSION
Think Like a Lawyer 109

APPENDIX

CAHILL CHART 113

EXCERPTS FROM PEOPLE v. CAHILL,
2 N.Y.3d 14 (2003) 117

INTRODUCTION

Congratulations. You've made it to law school. You've left behind the class-cutting, all-night-partying, socially-relevant-protesting, last-minute-cramming world of college, and you're ready to get serious. The problem is that if you study the same way you studied in college, even if you graduated with honors and wrote A-plus papers in your liberal arts subjects, you won't graduate with honors from law school or make the coveted law review. Why not? This book will answer that question. And in doing so, we will show you what you need to do in order to become not just a good lawyer but a great lawyer. And don't underestimate yourself: you can become a great lawyer. We can't do the work for you—you'll have to study as hard as you've ever studied in your life, and in a unique manner—but we can promise you that your efforts won't be wasted. Society needs great lawyers. Set your sights high and you will rise to the challenge.

What are you learning in law school? At first, lots of theoretical stuff about contracts and crimes and property. When the authors went to law school, that was about it—lots of theory, very little practice. In the last 20 years, there's been a sea-change in the way would-be lawyers are taught. Yes, you'll still suffer through the theory (you might even enjoy it), but the availability of practice-oriented courses and clinics, as well as part-time and summer internships at law firms and government offices, makes it possible for law students to get a much more realistic view of what the practice of law is really like.

In practice, lawyers are often said to be broadly divided into the litigators and the non-litigators. Each group has its quirks and its prejudices against the other. The litigators are supposed to be the brash, theatrical sort, trying to convince juries with their melodramatic flourishes; the non-litigators are the moles burrowing through wills and contracts and deeds.

But both groups have a common ground: every one of them knows—or should know—how to *think like a lawyer*. That's what you're in law school for. And whether you want to become a litigator or a real estate lawyer, it is essential that you understand that thinking like a lawyer means knowing *the art of argument*. Litigators have an obvious need for it. But even the non-litigators, who often find themselves negotiating with other lawyers in order to arrive at an agreement, must be able to construct sound arguments to support their position.

Constructing sound arguments requires little or no memorization. If you were a whiz in college because you were able to memorize vast amounts of material and recall it at will on multiple choice exams, your great memory will not carry you the distance in law school. Memorizing law outlines that break down "black-letter law" won't cut it. You have to be able to construct solid arguments by applying the law to different sets of facts. In this book we will teach you how to construct legal arguments using facts and law. Once you learn how to do that, you will be able to argue any legal issue, no matter what area of law.

When your law professors say, "*apply the law to the facts*," they simply mean, "*What is the legal significance of the facts you have been given?*" Facts take on legal significance because the law requires or sets a certain standard or test. The lawyer's job is to persuade the court or decision maker that the facts either meet the test or don't meet the test. So, the memo you draft or the law exam you write will usually involve two tasks: (1) analyze the law relevant to your issue; (2) apply that law to a set of facts. You'll usually be given facts in the form of a hypothetical or hypo: to solve any hypo you have to first research and analyze the relevant law, and then apply it, arguing both sides—showing why the legal test is or is not met in any given case. Usually law professors want you to argue both sides. But in the real world, as an advocate, you will take one side.

So, how do you use our book? After all, the goal is for you to transfer into your head what the authors have learned through decades of experience as prosecutors writing, arguing, and editing briefs and memoranda in state and federal trial and appellate courts. Our primary approach is to give you rules and also examples that show you how to apply those rules. Many of these examples are derived from a decision of the highest appellate court in the State of New York, the Court of Appeals, in which a divided court reversed a death sentence, and actual briefs filed in two first-degree murder appeals, materials that we feel are examples of superb legal thinking. We'll walk you through the relevant sections of each document. Along the way, we'll show you how the author of that document framed the legal issue, analyzed it, and constructed arguments to support the prosecution's position. We hope that by "looking over our shoulders" as we show you what great legal arguments are made of, you'll learn a method for constructing legal arguments—*to think like a lawyer.*

Finally, though, you will have to practice. You're learning a *craft*. In the end, you can only learn it by doing it. Like a surgeon practicing on a cadaver, you will have to practice answering hypos. Only by forcing yourself to tackle the difficult mental work of learning to construct your own arguments will you become the great lawyer that you want to be and that society needs you to be.

PART ONE:
THE BASICS

RULE ONE

Argument Is a Craft

Everyone thinks they know how to argue, because they do it nearly every day. But what most people don't realize is that argument, whether written or oral, is a craft that must be learned. Everything that follows in this book is designed to teach you that craft, and to supplement what you're already learning in law school. We teach you to *think like a lawyer*: to use a method of argument that, once mastered, will allow you to effectively argue your position in any litigation or dispute over any issue.

To make a written argument, a lawyer might simply write a letter. If court proceedings have already begun, the usual vehicle for argument is the memorandum of law (in support of, or in opposition to, some motion or application by one's opponent), or the brief (used on an appeal from a lower court ruling). In your law school experience, you've probably seen or written one of these before, or you will write one soon.

Throughout this book, we'll show you specific examples of the components of a written argument. But you'll soon understand that all properly written arguments share a common construction. That's right, *construction*, because the craft of argument is based upon the fundamental principle that arguments are constructed, piece by piece, and effective arguments all share a common structure. Once you learn the craft of argument, you won't need sample memoranda or briefs, because you'll be able to construct your own.

We've boiled the craft down to 46 essential rules. The contents of this book are organized around these rules, which form the chapter headings. Where appropriate, we illustrate a particular rule with examples taken from a New York Court of Appeals decision in a death penalty case, and briefs on appeal in two first-degree murder cases, all of which contain passages that nicely demonstrate the method we advocate in this book. The first group of 32 rules, in Parts One and Two, applies to constructing the analytical section of your argument: using factual and legal **contentions** to establish a claim. The second group of 14 rules, in Part Three, applies to narrating the **facts**. Although this might seem backwards to you at this point, we've found through experience that it's far easier to master the craft with this approach.

Remember, the rules we teach here apply both to oral and written arguments. They also apply to any situation where you need to be persuasive, whether in litigation or negotiation. For convenience, we'll generally refer to the "reader" or "judge" as the person you need to persuade, but bear in mind as you go along that the term applies to anyone to whom you're making your argument.

So, let's get started learning how to THINK LIKE A LAWYER!

RULE TWO

The Goal of Argument Is to Persuade

The goal of any argument, from your point of view, should be to persuade your reader—your professor, a moot court judge, your moot court opponent, the student on the other side of a clinical law negotiation—that you're right. Unfortunately, all too often law students and even lawyers throw this principle out the window and instead argue for the satisfaction of insulting their opponents. To be sure, there's a lot of satisfaction, albeit temporary, in directing witty barbs or personal attacks on the opposing party or counsel. But you gain nothing from such an attack; in fact, if your mind is occupied with barbs you won't be able to think analytically.

The craft of argument replaces childish venting with rational, goal-oriented action: the goal is to persuade. Persuasion results from proving that your position is right and just, and that your opponent's position is wrong and unjust. But you can't prove the rightness of your cause if you're flinging insults. All you'll do is lose credibility with the judge, and that could block your chances of winning.

RULE THREE

The Simple Declarative Sentence Is Your Best Weapon

Let's repeat that: the simple declarative sentence is your best weapon. Remember that grammar class you had in junior high school? The one you hated? Probably the easiest (and maybe only) principle you learned in that awful class was that of the simple declarative sentence: subject, verb, object, "The cat catches the mouse." Well, to master the craft of argument, you have only to make use of that basic language tool.

A key part of persuasion is making it as easy as possible for the person you are trying to win over to your point of view to understand the basis for your claim. Back in Dickens's time, lawyers judged their ability by the number of difficult words they could string together into tortured and incomprehensible sentences. Dickens satirized this practice in *David Copperfield.* In Mr. Micawber's scene of triumph against the slimy Uriah Heep, Micawber reads a letter accusing Heep of a variety of frauds, taking particular pride in such legalistic phrases as "To wit, in manner following, that is to say." The narrator remarks,

> Mr. Micawber had a relish in this formal piling up of words, which, however ludicrously displayed in his case, was, I must say, not at all peculiar to him . . . . In the taking of legal oaths, for instance, deponents seem to enjoy themselves mightily when they come to several good words in succession, for the expression of one idea; as, that they utterly detest, abominate, and abjure, or so forth . . . . We talk about the tyranny of words, but we like to tyrannise over them too; we

> are fond of having a large superfluous establishment of words to wait upon us on great occasions; we think it looks important, and sounds well . . . . [T]he meaning or necessity of our words is a secondary consideration, if there be but a great parade of them.

That is true no longer. Law schools now teach you future lawyers to write and speak in clear, easily digestible sentences consisting of simple nouns and active verbs. Legalese, once placed on the throne of legal discourse, is now dead. Simple English is now the mainstay of legal writing and argument. That is because simple declarative sentences are more persuasive than complicated legalese—even to other lawyers.

Here's the standard definition of a declarative sentence: a sentence that makes a statement. Simple enough. The particular type of declarative sentence that works best in constructing arguments is the **contention**. A contention is simply the point you're making. To use an everyday example: (a) You block my driveway every day. (b) When you block my driveway, I can't get my car out. (c) As a result, I'm late for work every day. As you can see, short, direct statements like these make your position plain. As we work our way through the rules, you'll discover that the craft of argument consists mainly of organizing these short, direct statements—your contentions—in the most logical and effective manner.

RULE FOUR

The More Complicated the Argument, The Simpler Your Presentation Should Be

This may sound like a paradox, but it isn't. Why? Because the subject matter of the argument, whether complicated or simple, is wholly separate and distinct from your presentation of the argument itself. Whether your issue involves a simple rule of black-letter law, or a complicated and novel issue, the presentation of your argument must be simple and easy to follow. In fact, if you construct your argument properly, the reader will so easily digest it that he or she won't even have to read it twice, let alone struggle to understand what you mean. Once you master the craft of argument, you'll be able to "spoon-feed" your argument to your reader, no matter how difficult or complex the subject matter.

RULE FIVE

Before You Write or State Your Argument, You Must Be Sure What It Is

You're probably thinking that this rule is dumb. After all, how can you state or write an argument if you don't know what it is? Exactly. Yet, too often you may be tempted to rush to speak up in class or answer an exam question or draft a brief or memorandum of law without first knowing exactly what you're going to say or write. In your zeal to show how much knowledge you've amassed, you end up losing points because you haven't organized your thoughts first.

The way to avoid this embarrassment is to take the time to build your argument, step by step, so that you can argue your position in a logical, persuasive manner. As a law student, you must learn to think clearly and under pressure—but that doesn't mean you should say or write whatever comes into your head. That's what amateurs do, and you're in law school to become a professional.

RULE SIX

Stream of Consciousness Has No Place in Your Argument

Take the time to think before you respond either orally or in writing. Thinking on your feet does not mean saying (or writing) the first thing that comes into your mind. You've studied your law books until your eyes hurt and your mind is crammed with outlines and cases. Resist the temptation to go straight to your memory; even if you take only a few seconds, if you're called upon in class force yourself to organize your thoughts in your head or on paper before answering. And, before you write an exam answer or memorandum of law, first jot down an outline of the argument you want to make. Your goal is to build your argument from its most basic, logical pieces: **contentions**. Once those pieces are organized, your argument will come together in a smooth, logical flow that is far more powerful than unfocused thoughts, no matter how rooted those thoughts may be in your familiarity with the course materials. Stream of consciousness is as about as effective as driving your car blindfolded. You'll crash, your argument will fall apart, and ultimately, your grades will suffer.

When you're called upon in class, the professor wants you to respond with an argument, or at least an analysis of the relevant arguments pertaining to your issue. No more liberal-arts-class rambles about the class struggle, please. You need to be able to zero in on the pertinent legal and/or factual issues with surgical precision, or you'll be wasting everybody's time, including your own. Likewise, when you answer a long hypo on an exam, the grader will be scoring you on the quality of your arguments, or your analysis of the arguments relevant to the issues, not your ability to write a social critique. Your free-range, metaphysical musings might fascinate your friends, but in the real world they're not likely to persuade anybody.

Bottom line: don't ever say or write just whatever comes into your head. Organize first.

RULE SEVEN

An Argument May Be Legal, Factual, or Both

From your first day in law school, you've been given court decisions to read and analyze. Obviously, these decisions concern factual or legal disputes. If the decision is well drafted, it will thoroughly review all the claims raised by the appellant as well as the respondent's opposition to those claims. If you're digesting these decisions solely to memorize the black-letter law relied upon by the court, you're ignoring the protein and stuffing yourself with the fat. In reading and analyzing decisions, break them down into the factual and legal contentions made by the parties. Then separately digest the court's response to each of those contentions. You'll notice that often the court itself, in accepting or rejecting those contentions, argues each claim before stating its ultimate conclusion. Breaking down the decisions into separate arguments will help you learn to construct your own arguments, your ultimate goal.

You may have heard the old lawyers' adage: if you don't have the law on your side, argue the facts; if you don't have the facts on your side, argue the law; and if you don't have either the law or the facts, pound on the podium. Our method is designed to teach you how to use the law, or the facts, or both to your best advantage—without having to pound on the podium.

FACT PATTERN FOR THE EXAMPLES

We've chosen a death penalty case from New York State, ***People v. Cahill***, 2 N.Y.3d 14 (2003), to illustrate many of the rules of argument construction. An appeal from a death sentence to the highest New York State appeals court, the Court of Appeals, *Cahill* is unusual because the judges on the court split on a critical issue: the weight of the evidence as to Cahill's guilt of capital murder. As you'll see when we break it down, that issue was hotly debated by the majority, which voted to reverse Cahill's death sentence, and the dissenters, who attacked the majority's conclusions with unusual bitterness. The split decision, however, makes *Cahill* a perfect subject for dissection because both sides were forced to defend their respective positions. In doing so, the judges on the court, all brilliant and experienced jurists, demonstrate the art of using **Main Contentions** and supporting factual and legal contentions as deftly as samurai warriors battling with swords. We've broken down the main contentions related to the battle over Cahill's guilt of witness elimination murder, a capital crime, into a chart that you'll find in the Appendix. We'll be referring to the chart throughout the rest of the book, as the contentions shown there clearly illustrate the rules of argument we want you to learn to use. So, take a look at the chart now, but don't try to read it for information at this point; its primary usefulness will become apparent as we move through the rest of the rules.

The basic facts of the case were that in early April, 1998, **James Cahill** and his wife, **Jill**, legally separated, but continued to live in the same house in upstate New York. On April 21st, during an argument, Cahill hit his wife repeatedly in the head with a baseball bat. Jill cried out to their two young children, telling them to call the police because their father was trying to kill her. After the attack, Cahill called his parents for help. They came to the house, as did the police, who found Jill lying on the kitchen floor, covered in blood, writhing in pain, and moaning incoherently. Her left temple was visibly damaged. Cahill, on the other hand, had minor cuts and scratches.

Cahill and his wife were taken to different hospitals. Following treatment, James Cahill was taken to the police station. He told the police his wife had started the argument and then attacked him with a knife, causing cuts and scratches; he claimed he hit her in self-defense. He later admitted that he hit her with the bat when she was not armed, and that he cut himself to make it look like self-defense.

In June, 1998, Cahill was indicted for first-degree assault and criminal possession of a weapon in the fourth degree. Meanwhile, custody proceedings began in Family Court, which placed the Cahill children with their maternal grandparents and aunt. Orders of protection prohibiting Cahill from seeing his children or entering his wife's hospital room were also issued by the Family Court.

Jill Cahill's injuries from the baseball bat attack showed that she had been hit at least four times in the head. After undergoing brain surgery to remove a blood clot from her brain, she suffered from brain swelling and a number of life-threatening infections. She improved and was moved to the coma rehabilitation unit and then the general rehabilitation unit. By October of 1998, seven months after the assault, Jill Cahill was able to recall the names of her children and regained some ability to speak, but could use only short, simple words.

On October 27, 1998, after the hospital was closed to visitors, James Cahill entered the hospital disguised as a maintenance worker. He went into his wife's room and forced cyanide down her throat. He had ordered the cyanide over the Internet, pretending to represent a local manufacturing company, and had intercepted delivery of the cyanide by posing as a company employee. Jill Cahill died the next morning of cyanide poisoning.

James Cahill was arrested for the murder, and police recovered data from his computer showing that he had ordered cyanide. They also found on his property a half-burned wig and a bottle containing cyanide. Eyewitnesses identified him as the person who had intercepted delivery of the cyanide.

Cahill was indicted on two counts of first-degree murder. One charged him with having murdered Jill Cahill to prevent her from testifying against him at his trial for the April 1998 baseball bat assault. The second count charged him with committing the murder during his commission of a burglary, that is, his entering the hospital, during off-hours and in disguise, with the intent to poison Jill Cahill once inside her room.

At trial, the jury found him guilty of both first-degree murder counts, and then, after a penalty phase, the jury sentenced him to death on both counts. He later appealed to the New York State Court of Appeals, claiming that the prosecution had failed to prove both that he intended to eliminate Jill Cahill as a witness and that he committed a burglary.

RULE EIGHT

Contentions Are the Building Blocks of an Argument

Back in Rule Three we touched on the major role that **contentions**—expressed in simple declarative sentences—play in arguments. Let's revisit that now: A contention is an assertion put forward in an argument. In other words, it's the point—legal or factual—that you're making. Here's a legal contention: A city ordinance makes it illegal to block someone's driveway. (This cites the law.) Now, look at a factual contention: You block my driveway every day. (This simply states a fact.) We've said it earlier, but this is so important we have to repeat it: The craft of argument consists of **organizing contentions** in the most effective manner.

From here on out, everything that follows will build upon the cornerstone of any properly constructed argument, **the contention**. That sounds simple enough. We all know what a contention is. Similarly, we all know when someone is arguing effectively as opposed to spouting nonsense. But knowing something intellectually and doing it well are two very different animals. Practically everyone knows when a movie is good or bad, but only skilled artists are capable of actually making a good movie. Merely knowing what contentions are doesn't mean you can automatically know how to use them effectively; you need the skill to use them to construct your argument effectively.

All the rules that follow focus on this problem by teaching you this skill. Effective arguments, like any other structured creation, are the result of discipline and self-imposed limitations.

In order to master the craft of argument, you must become adept at shaping your thoughts according to rigid rules of organization. In formulating arguments, contentions bring order out of chaos: they form disorganized thoughts into weapons of logic.

RULE NINE

A Contention Is a Positive Statement That Can Be Made in One Sentence

There are two absolutes in Rule Nine that you must adhere to: *positive statement* and *one sentence*. It is possible, of course, to make a positive statement in more than one sentence, even more than one paragraph. But for purposes of building an argument, you must arbitrarily limit each contention to one sentence. By limiting yourself in this way, you are forced to reduce your position down to its most basic elements. Needless to say, in doing so, you'll automatically squeeze flabby blobs of verbiage into tightly compressed declarative sentences that state a positive in an effective, compelling manner. So, in making your argument, whether written or oral, never make a contention that can't be expressed in one sentence.

Naturally, your final written argument isn't going to consist of only a list of one-sentence contentions. As you develop your argument, you're going to expand on the contentions by proving them right, step by step, using both the facts and the law. But, before you do, by practicing the discipline of reducing the essence of each contention to a single sentence, you will make a clear, concise argument out of a mass of disconnected ideas.

EXAMPLE

In *Cahill*, the main factual **contentions** for the majority and the dissent were, in a nutshell, as follows:

- **MAJORITY:** The evidence showed only that Cahill poisoned his wife because she wanted to divorce him, not to eliminate her as a witness against him at his upcoming trial.

- **DISSENT:** The evidence showed that a substantial factor in Cahill's killing of his wife was his desire to eliminate her as a witness at his upcoming trial.

As you'll see later, both the majority and the dissent expertly **proved** these contentions using exactly the methods we recommend here, step by step, through skillful, organized use of both the law and the facts.

RULE TEN

Your Contentions Must Prove Your Main Argument

Let's start with a new term: **Main Argument**. This is the bedrock claim that you want to make in your argument. If you're arguing or analyzing the plaintiff's side, it's what you (or the plaintiff) wants satisfied. For example, suppose Mr. Aggrieved has a neighbor, Mr. Rogers, with a young son who fancies himself another Roger Clemens. The kid has thrown a baseball through Mr. Aggrieved's front window. Mr. Aggrieved wants reimbursement from Mr. Rogers for the cost of repairing the window. So, the Main Argument for the plaintiff would go something like this: Mr. Rogers's son broke Mr. Aggrieved's window with a baseball. Therefore, Mr. Rogers is liable to pay for the damage his son caused.

As shown in the simple example above, the Main Argument for the plaintiff must state not only the plaintiff's grievance (the son broke the window), but must incorporate also the remedy (pay for the damages) that the plaintiff seeks. The whole point of your argument is to obtain or get satisfaction in the form of a tangible remedy. It's not enough to simply make it known that the plaintiff is unhappy about something. That's not a claim for purposes of argument. Nor is insulting your opponent or bringing up unrelated complaints. The Main Argument, whether for the plaintiff or the defendant, must be as narrow and specific as you can make it.

Unlike a contention, the Main Argument can be expressed in more than one sentence. (We'll get to the technique for actually formulating your Main Argument later.) Now that we've defined Main Argument, we can talk about the relationship between your contentions and your Main Argument. Simply put, **your**

contentions prove your Main Argument. That's right: an argument is nothing more or less than a way of proving that your Main Argument is valid, through contentions organized in a compelling and persuasive manner. Exactly how you go about organizing your contentions will be discussed in the rules that follow.

EXAMPLE

Take a look at the ***Cahill* Chart** in the Appendix. You'll see that the **fourth box** down for each column is captioned **Factual Contentions that "Prove" Main Argument**. Below that are boxes captioned FC1-FC8 for the Majority and FC1-FC9 for the Dissent. Each of those is a factual contention that "proves" or supports the majority's or the dissent's Main Argument.

RULE ELEVEN

Arrange Your Contentions In Descending Order of Importance

The architecture of your contentions must follow one basic scheme: arrange them in *descending order of importance*. Why? Because you'll be most likely to grab the reader's attention quickly if you start with the most compelling facts and/or the most authoritative rules (the legal contentions we mentioned back in Rules Eight and Nine) that support your Main Argument. In a law school setting, because your reader (a professor or exam grader or moot court judge) will be judging the quality of your written or oral arguments, he will be listening to or reading your responses as if he were a decision-maker. Your goal, then, must be to present, orally or in writing, the most effective arguments possible. This requires not only that you be thorough and accurate, but also that you present your arguments in a persuasive manner.

So, start by deciding on your Main Argument: what does the party whose side you are arguing *really want*? Why is he or she entitled to this remedy? Then, make a list of all the contentions, factual and legal, that you believe will prove your Main Argument. Look it over carefully. What's the most important contention? Put yourself in the shoes of the reader and determine, objectively, which contention would be the most persuasive, then the second most persuasive, and so on, until you've reordered the entire list. If it's a law exam, repeat the process for the other party.

Now look at the bottom of each list: Are there any contentions there that are irrelevant or unnecessary? Don't be afraid to prune them out. When you're making an argument, the more is not necessarily the merrier. Throwing in every fact, no matter how insignificant, will only weaken your argument by boring and/or confusing the reader.

The process of listing and sorting your contentions will give you the spine upon which to build your arguments. In a sense, you'll be constructing your arguments from the inside out.

EXAMPLE

Looking again at the FC boxes on the ***Cahill* Chart**, FC 1 for each side is the most important contention supporting that side's Main Argument. The majority made FC-1 the linchpin of its argument because the judges concluded that the single most powerful piece of evidence demonstrating that Cahill killed his wife because she wanted to divorce him was that he procured the cyanide long before there was any basis to think that Jill Cahill could ever testify against him.

On the dissent side of the bench, the judges felt that the evidence of Cahill's motivation established that he wanted to stop her from challenging his version of the truth about the baseball bat attack. In other words, the dissenters felt that it was more important to Cahill to preserve his children's image of him as a father than to kill a potential witness to the assault.

From their respective choices of first factual contentions, it is clear that each side saw the same facts in a completely different light, leading to diametrically opposite conclusions. But they did not stop there. They each discussed, in descending order of importance, the additional facts that tended to prove the conclusion they had come to. Each new fact added something to the preceding one, until a compelling argument emerged.

RULE TWELVE

A Contention Should Be The Topic Sentence of Every Paragraph

Remember the "topic sentence" from ninth-grade English composition? The definition of a topic sentence, as one old grammar book puts it, is, "The sentence within a paragraph that states the main thought, often placed at the beginning." Regardless of which side you are arguing, once you've decided upon your Main Argument and listed all the contentions you'll be relying upon to prove that claim in order of descending importance, you'll have the skeleton of your argument. When you actually start writing out your argument, your contentions will become the topic sentences of your paragraphs.

To give your argument maximum effectiveness, you must rigidly streamline it: Each and every paragraph must start with a topic sentence that states a contention. That's right: Each and every paragraph should begin with one of your contentions. Your paragraphs will also be organized in descending order of importance, reflecting the relative importance of the contentions that begin them.

Likewise, if you're doing a moot court oral argument, or even answering a hypo orally in class, you'll want to structure your presentation so that you're able, from the outset, to state your Main Argument and each of the contentions that you're going to rely upon to prove your Main Argument. These will be the "talking points" that guide you through your oral presentation. Again, you should be prepared to orally argue each of your talking points in descending order of importance.

Wait a minute, you're thinking. How can I prepare in advance to answer some surprise hypo in class? The answer is that once you've mastered the techniques outlined in this book, you'll have gotten yourself into the habit of organizing contentions automatically. A class hypo is usually short and designed to illustrate just one or two principles of law, so, once you've gotten into that habit, it should be a snap for you to quickly think through your talking points before you open your mouth.

For moot court purposes, you don't want to stand and read from your notes. When you prepare for your moot court argument, you'll structure your preparation by reviewing all of your talking points. Then, when responding to questions from the moot court judges, you'll use, without looking down and reading from your notes, the contentions that make up the proof for your Main Argument. Although you may appear to be thinking on your feet, your answers will in reality have been thought out in advance, and you'll have been able to anticipate most, if not all, of the questions you are asked. If you ask any seasoned lawyer the secret of great trial or appellate advocacy, they will tell you *preparation, preparation, preparation*. But you have to know how to prepare. That requires that you outline in advance your Main Argument and all of the talking points that prove your Main Argument.

EXAMPLE

If you look at the majority opinion in *Cahill*, you'll see that the section dealing with the issue of the weight of the evidence on the witness-elimination murder count is written like an argument in a brief. To that end, each paragraph begins with a topic sentence containing a factual contention that further proves the main contention: that James Cahill's motive was not witness elimination. Here are the majority's topic sentences:

- "First, the May 1998 Family Court appearances primarily concerned the Cahill children."
- "Using the prosecution's timeline, a critical feature refutes its witness elimination theory: defendant procured potassium cyanide long before there was any possible belief—on

anyone's part—that Jill could ever testify at a trial, given her condition."

- "In seeking to prove that defendant knew Jill was able to speak and was afraid of what she would say, the People relied largely on the testimony of Patricia Cahill, defendant's mother. She merely testified, however, that defendant told her that 'I hope when this is all concluded that she can tell the truth about what led to the break-up of their marriage.'"
- "Additional factors rebut the witness elimination theory. The very brutality of the April 1998 assault permits the compelling inference that, even as of then, defendant wanted to kill his wife and that ultimately doing so fulfilled his previously formed intent, which sprang from the impending divorce."
- "Beyond that, defendant had fully confessed to the assault and the prosecution had a powerful case without Jill's testimony."

As you can see, careful use of topic sentences can make a "powerful case" out of a mass of facts. Their prominent place at the beginning of each paragraph draws the reader's attention immediately, so that even a "skimmer" will quickly get the sense of the argument.

RULE THIRTEEN

The Body of Each Paragraph Should Prove The Truth of Its Topic Sentence Contention

Just as each contention must prove the Main Argument, each paragraph must prove the contention that forms its topic sentence. How do you prove a contention? With the facts or law that support your position. Your topic sentence contention will be either fact-based or law-based or both. You'll then back up your topic-sentence contention by arguing those particular facts or legal principles that support your contention. Restricting yourself to these guidelines will eliminate any possibility of excess verbiage cluttering up your argument. Your contentions will merge into a seamless, streamlined whole that will give you your best shot at persuading the reader or moot court judge that your Main Argument is valid.

The same guidelines apply to your oral presentation: think of each one of your talking points as a "topic sentence." Your oral presentation should be guided by the particular facts or legal principles that support each talking point. Since you will have also outlined the Main Argument and talking points that your opponent will likely use, along with your response to each of those points, you should be able to respond to questions from the judges that encompass your opponent's arguments.

EXAMPLE

One of the critical focal points of the "debate" between the majority and dissenting Judge Graffeo in *Cahill* concerned the timeline of Cahill's actions leading up to his poisoning his wife. Below we print, *verbatim*, a brief section of the majority opinion that argues its view of these crucial facts. Notice how the majority starts off by stating a contention, and how the remainder of the paragraph consists of specific factual contentions that support that assertion.

Excerpt from Judge Rosenblatt's majority opinion:

> [Contention:] **Using the prosecution's timeline, a critical feature refutes its witness elimination theory: defendant procured potassium cyanide long before there was any possible belief—on anyone's part—that Jill could ever testify at a trial, given her condition.** [Fact 1:] After the assault, Jill suffered from a host of medical complications that utterly incapacitated her as a witness. [**Fact 2:**] Further, one doctor testified that as late as August 1998, when Jill entered the coma rehabilitation unit, her cognitive abilities ranked at a five or six on a 25-point scale. [**Fact 3:**] Moreover, at the corresponding criminal proceedings, there was no mention that Jill might or possibly could testify against defendant. [**Fact 4:**] Indeed, there is not a shred of evidence in this record that Jill had even retained a memory of the assault. [**Fact 5:**] Most compellingly, an Assistant District Attorney testified that up to the date of Jill's murder no law enforcement official had even interviewed her about the assault.

2 N.Y.3d at 60 (footnote omitted; emphasis added).

Judge Rosenblatt's attack on the prosecution position is effective because it is *organized.* He affirmatively states his main contention, and then backs it up with fact after fact, until even a hostile reader is forced to acknowledge that his argument is strong.

RULE FOURTEEN

The Last Sentence of Each Paragraph Should Nail the Proof into the Reader's Mind

You should never end a paragraph in your argument without a concluding contention. Always keep in mind that the sole purpose of your argument is to persuade the judge that your Main Argument is valid. Argument writing is as different from ordinary communication as solving math problems is from writing a novel. Your argument isn't meant to entertain; it's a weapon you use to win the particular battle you're engaged in. In each paragraph, you make your contention, you prove it, and then you end by telling the reader or judge what you've proven in that paragraph. Leave nothing to chance; use the last sentence of each paragraph to nail down what you've proven in that paragraph.

This rule is just as important in oral argument. Clarity is the single most important aspect of any oral presentation. Whatever point you are trying to make, it won't come across unless you are clear. And you can't be clear unless you are organized. Remember, any oral presentation involves following a path that you have already set down for yourself. Your goal is to lead your listener down that path, point by point, until you reach the conclusion you want your listener to adopt. In oral argument, even if you are barraged with questions, and have little opportunity to make an uninterrupted statement, you use the judge's questions to get your points across. Just as in your written argument, each talking point should state a contention, which you then prove by weaving factual and legal contentions together, and end by telling the judge what you've proven in that point of your argument.

EXAMPLE

One of the majority's key factual contentions in *Cahill* is that Cahill had no reason to kill his wife to prevent her from testifying at his assault trial, because he had fully confessed to the crime. In the paragraph quoted below, notice how the last sentence of the paragraph plays off the first sentence, driving home the point of the paragraph. This single paragraph is a masterful example in and of itself of the craft of argument.

Excerpt from Judge Rosenblatt's majority opinion:

> [Contention:] **Beyond that, defendant had fully confessed to the assault and the prosecution had a powerful case without Jill's testimony.** [**Facts:**] In confessing to the assault, defendant admitted that he hit Jill on the head at least three or four times with the baseball bat. He further admitted that he struck her while she was unarmed, thus foreclosing any plausible calm of self-defense. He also confessed to having wounded himself, a deception designed to make it look as if he acted in self-defense, and that he attempted suicide after the assault. [**Conclusion:**] **In light of these candid disclosures, there is scant basis to believe that defendant thought he could avoid an assault conviction by murdering Jill.**

2 N.Y.3d at 61-62 (emphasis added).

Right at the start, Judge Rosenblatt states what he clearly believes is a powerful factual contention: "defendant had fully confessed to the assault and the prosecution had a powerful case without Jill's testimony." The rest of the paragraph, up until the final sentence, proves that contention by detailing the contents of the confession. The last sentence begins with a wrap-up transition, "In light of these candid disclosures," that leads into the final thrust: "there is scant basis to believe that defendant thought he could avoid an assault conviction by murdering Jill." Notice, too, how Judge Rosenblatt uses understatement to drive home his point by using the phrase "scant basis." Make no mistake, this is written argument at its highest level.

RULE FIFTEEN

The Last Sentence of Each Paragraph Should Lead into the Next Topic Sentence Contention

You know where you're going with your argument, but the reader doesn't. Once you've caught the reader's attention, you want to make your argument unfold so smoothly that it's virtually spoon-fed, a little at a time, in easy stages. The reader should be able to digest each step in the argument's progression without stopping to think. There should be no confusion. If the reader has to stop and struggle to figure out what you're trying to say, then you've lost ground. The argument should flow uninterrupted to its logical conclusion, and, ideally, the reader shouldn't even be aware that he or she is following you down a well constructed path.

The way to maintain the uninterrupted flow of your argument is by using the first sentence of each paragraph as a transition from the previous concluding contention. A paragraph must never simply begin, without any tangible relationship to the previous conclusion. Otherwise, the argument will be broken into pieces, losing much of its power.

EXAMPLE

Look again at the example for the previous rule, this time with an eye to the key transition phrases that Judge Rosenblatt uses both at the beginning of the paragraph ("Beyond that") and to start the last crucial sentence ("In light of these candid disclosures"). He demonstrates that transition phrases are more than mere mechanical devices; when used skillfully they provide the connective tissue for your argument.

CAUTION: Transition words are no substitute for actual logical transitions. You can't simply use words like "indeed" or "moreover" to tie completely unrelated contentions together. If you find yourself doing that, then take another look at your contention list: Are the contentions in the right order? Are any of them unnecessary? (See Part I, Rule Eleven.) Don't cheat on this, for you'll only be cheating your argument—and yourself.

PART TWO: THE COMPLEX ARGUMENT

RULE SIXTEEN

The Point Is the Basic Organizing Tool Of Your Brief

In Part One, we showed you the fundamentals of persuasive writing—the use of contentions to state and then prove your Main Argument. But the exam hypos you will get and the cases you are studying present complex fact patterns, involving several arguments on multiple issues. How do you construct arguments when presented with complicated fact patterns? Read on.

A complex fact pattern requires that you argue multiple issues. That means that your argument should be subdivided into sub-arguments. You'll still have one, overarching Main Argument; but for the sake of clarity, if you find that you have to advance several unique positions, some of which might be in the alternative, then you should further subdivide your argument into additional points, one for each sub-argument.

Wait just a second, you're probably saying. What's all this about sub-arguments and additional points? What is a "point" anyhow, and why haven't we mentioned it before now? Let's pause to define sub-argument and point. If your Main Argument goes beyond one issue you need to break it down for your reader into subsections. Each of those subsections should focus on a sub-argument, a claim or issue that is important enough to deserve its own subheading in your brief, memorandum of law, or exam answer, but which still fits into the Main Argument. Each sub-argument will be organized using **the point** as the basic organizing tool. Sometimes several sub-arguments will be included in a single point; or, a sub-argument may be given its own separate point. We haven't mentioned the "point" until now because for learning purposes, you have to understand how to draft a simple argument first.

Whether you have one or more points, each point will follow the same basic structure, which we'll discuss below.

EXAMPLE

Printed below is the actual point heading from the prosecution's brief in *Cahill* for its point arguing that Cahill's conviction for witness elimination murder was supported by legally sufficient evidence and was not against the weight of the evidence. Needless to say, the text of the point itself followed the structure presented in the table of contents. Notice how the prosecution broke its two-part Main Argument down into two separate sub-arguments, labeled by sub-headings. In doing so, the prosecution chose to first present its legal argument that the statute defining first-degree murder did not require that the prosecution prove that witness elimination was the sole motive. Then, in a separate sub-argument, the prosecution argued that the evidence at trial proved that one purpose of the killing was to prevent Jill Cahill's testimony. That sub-argument was, in turn, broken down into four sub-contentions, each with its own sub-heading. The majority, in rejecting the prosecution's view of the case, felt compelled to specifically answer each of the prosecution's factual contentions, set forth in subsection B(1)-(4) of its point. In other words, even though the prosecution ultimately lost on this point, its main argument, broken down into two sub-arguments, was effective enough to require serious consideration; and, indeed, their main argument convinced the dissenters.

POINT XII

APPELLANT'S CONVICTION FOR A WITNESS-ELIMINATION MURDER WAS BASED UPON LEGALLY SUFFICIENT EVIDENCE AND WAS NOT AGAINST THE WEIGHT OF THE EVIDENCE

A. Penal Law § 125.27(1)(a)(v) Does Not Require The People To Prove That Witness Elimination Was The Exclusive Motive For the Murder.
B. The Evidence At Trial Was Legally Sufficient To Establish That The Murder Was Committed For The Purpose Of Preventing The Testimony Of A Witness.

1. On The Dates That Appellant's Case Is Discussed In Family Court, He Researched Cyanide On The Internet And Methods Of Procuring The Poison.
2. Further Developments In Appellant's Criminal Case Coincide With His Procurement of Cyanide.
3. Soon After Learning That His Mother Has Visited Jill Cahill In The Hospital And That The Victim Was Capable Of Speaking, Appellant Was Observed In Disguise In Jill's Hospital Room.
4. Appellant Returned To The Hospital One Week Later And Poisoned The Victim, Only Days Before A Hearing Regarding The Admissibility Of His Confession.

Note how these point headings neatly lay out the prosecution's contentions. When you make your list of contentions in preparation for writing an argument, that list can serve as a handy basis for the headings and sub-headings in the brief later on.

RULE SEVENTEEN

Set Up Your Points

You have to set up your points before you actually write them. Whether you use only one point, or multiple points, the actual set up of each point will be the same, structurally. As you've probably figured out by now, a simple argument is constructed of one point, while a complex one may have two, three, or more points. But a point is like your audio system. It's built from several different components, but you don't use all the components to listen to music. Similarly, you don't have to use all of the available components in every point. You'll typically use only those components that are necessary to your individual set of facts and the particular contentions that you're making. But to start, we will discuss all the possible components that are available to you when setting up a point.

Here's how to set up each of your points, in a nutshell:

1. Start your point with an intro paragraph. In a simple argument, which may be limited to just a single point, this will just be a couple of sentences letting the reader know the gist of your Main Argument. In a more complex argument, with multiple points, you'll need to summarize, in each separate point, the sub-argument central to that point, and a bit of the background. We'll explain this in more detail in Rule Eighteen.
2. Next, you'll need what we call a law paragraph (or section). This summarizes the legal principles that apply to your Main Argument. If your Main Argument is broken down into sub-arguments, each with its own point, then each of

those points will have its own law section summarizing the legal principles germane to that particular sub-argument. Rules Nineteen through Twenty-Four will show you how to write your law paragraph effectively.

3. After you've laid out the applicable law, you can begin to affirmatively prove your claim by applying the law to your facts. You'll see in Rules Twenty-Five and Twenty-Six the best way to do this.
4. Now you can deal with your opponent's contentions, if necessary. Rules Twenty-Seven through Thirty outline the dos and don'ts of refuting your opponent's arguments and factual allegations.
5. Finally, end your point with a conclusion paragraph that sums up your position, as we'll show you in Rule Thirty-One.

EXAMPLE

Take another look at the ***Cahill* chart** in the Appendix, but this time look at the ***structure*** of the arguments made by the majority and Judge Graffeo's dissent. You'll see that both constructed their respective arguments on the issue of weight of the evidence for witness elimination murder in a way that mirrors the point structure we've given you in this rule. Their treatment of the issue in each instance could even be a "point" if it were separated from the rest of each opinion and presented as part of a brief or memorandum of law. Of course, both Judge Rosenblatt's majority opinion and Judge Graffeo's dissent were drafted by masters of the craft of argument, so each reflects the unique style and approach of its author. But the core of their arguments is built upon the classic point structure we've provided for you in this rule.

RULE EIGHTEEN

The Intro Paragraph Frames the Issue

In a brief or memorandum of law, or even in your answer to an exam question, the intro paragraph frames the issue for the reader. Often, the way an issue is framed determines the resolution, so if you can persuade the reader to define the issue your way, he or she will be more inclined to accept your argument and your conclusion. At a minimum, the intro paragraph must focus the reader on the essence of your main argument and the relief you're seeking. One or two sentences will usually accomplish this task. In other instances, it will be necessary to briefly summarize the factual background before stating your main argument. In a complex argument with multiple points, the intro paragraph of each point will frame the sub-argument of that point.

EXAMPLE

Below is an excerpt from an appellate brief written by the co-author of this book, Linda Cantoni, on behalf of the prosecution in a first-degree murder case, *People v. Bell*, 307 A.D.2d 1047, 763 N.Y.S.2d 762 (2d Dept. 2003). One of the defendant's claims on appeal was that the trial court's instruction to the jury on reasonable doubt misstated the correct law. Answering this claim in a point captioned "**THE TRIAL COURT'S REASONABLE DOUBT CHARGE WAS PROPER**," Ms. Cantoni begins the point with the following intro paragraph:

> In its final instructions to the jury on reasonable doubt, the trial court properly explained that a reasonable doubt is one

> that "a reasonable person acting in a matter of this importance would be likely to entertain"; that it is "a doubt for which some reason can be given"; and that the jury's first duty was to weigh all the evidence and then determine if a reasonable doubt exists (Charge: 13302-04). These instructions, along with the court's instructions on the presumption of innocence and the prosecution's burden to prove defendant's guilt beyond a reasonable doubt, neither "diluted" the prosecution's burden, nor shifted it to defendant. Nevertheless, defendant claims that these instructions improperly obligated the jurors to affirmatively articulate a reason for any doubt of guilt, and put the onus on the defense to supply reasonable doubt. Defendant is wrong.

Analysis of intro paragraph:

This intro paragraph begins with two affirmative contentions. The first one—the first sentence of the paragraph—incorporates the necessary factual background with brief quotes from the trial court's instruction at issue. The second contention focuses the reader on the narrow question—whether the quoted instructions diluted the prosecution's burden of proof or shifted that burden to the defendant—while also providing the answer to that question. Finally, the last sentence specifically delineates the defendant's claim and denies it.

In just three sentences, this intro paragraph accomplishes the goal of framing the issue, providing a glimpse at the affirmative argument that will be at the core of the point, and identifying the defendant's claim while attacking it as incorrect. By the time the reader finishes this short paragraph, she has been given a full preview of the contents of the point. She knows *how* the prosecution defines the issue, the core of the prosecution's affirmative contentions in the point, and its response to the defendant's claim.

Note that the intro paragraph could have been written without any quotes from the trial court's instructions. Read it again, striking out the quotes. In this instance, Ms. Cantoni felt that the brief quotations containing the court's actual reasonable doubt instruction fit neatly into the intro paragraph because they conclusively proved, from the record, that the court gave correct instructions. Other times, you may conclude that there is no reason to include specific quotes or other facts at this early juncture. If you do use them, do so sparingly at this point—you want to keep your intro paragraph clean and uncluttered, so that the reader can see instantly what your argument is.

RULE NINETEEN

The Procedural Contention Should Stand Alone

Unlike all the other elements of your point, the procedural contention stands alone. It has nothing to do with whether the claim itself is a winner or a loser, but it can make the difference between winning or losing the case. In short, a procedural contention is what is popularly known as a "technicality": your opponent may be barred from even making his claim, whatever its merits.

The bar may relate to time (like the statute of limitations, which limits how long someone can wait before filing a lawsuit) or some other failure to follow the technical rules applicable to your particular dispute. For example, a basic rule for making most types of claims on an appeal is that the claim has to have been "preserved" at trial; in other words, the person has to have complained to the trial judge first and given that judge a chance to rule on the issue, in order to be entitled to get an appellate court to review the claim. So, you may be able to argue that your opponent can't get appellate review because he or she didn't preserve the claim for appeal.

Other procedural bars, as they're called, may arise from a party's waiver of an issue. For example, a criminal defendant who pleads guilty generally waives his right to claim later that he is innocent. And many defendants who plead guilty sign a waiver of appeal, by which they give up their right to bring any issues in their case before an appellate court. In a civil case, the plaintiff may have, before filing the lawsuit, given the defendant a release of liability. There are numerous kinds of procedural bars that can be raised to prevent an opponent from even making his claim at all.

So, the procedural contention will have nothing to do with the substantive arguments that you make later in your argument.

It is completely independent of those contentions. Even if you have a procedural contention that you believe is a winner, or that will determine the outcome of the case (a real case, or a moot court case, or an exam hypo), you must still continue on and make your substantive arguments. You want the decision maker to decide in your favor on *both* procedural and substantive grounds. You can't have too many reasons for winning.

Your procedural contention properly goes *before* your attack on the merits of your opponent's claim. It's what courts usually call a "threshold" issue. Think of a procedural bar as a locked door. Your opponent can't cross the "threshold" if the door is locked. But remember, the court may disagree with you on the procedural contention, and may unlock that door. That's why you must move on to rest of your argument, which will deal with the merits of the claim.

By the same token, if your opponent is arguing that *you* are barred from making a claim on some procedural ground, you must dispose of that argument first. No matter how meritorious your claim, it won't do you any good if the court won't even entertain it because you failed to overcome a procedural bar first.

EXAMPLE

Below is an excerpt from an appellate brief written by the co-author of this book, Gary Fidel, on behalf of the prosecution in a first-degree murder case, *People v. Godineaux*, 2 A.D.3d 875, 769 N.Y.S.2d 744 (2d Dept. 2003). The defendant claimed that his guilty plea to first-degree murder had been coerced. In his answer to this claim, Mr. Fidel invoked a procedural bar in a section of his single-point argument:

Defendant's Claims, Whether Record-Based Or Outside The Scope of The Record, Are Unpreserved For Appellate Review.

The record demonstrates that defendant did not give the trial court an opportunity to correct alleged errors in the plea proceedings.

He made no motion to withdraw his guilty plea pursuant to C.P.L 220.60 (3), nor did he make a motion to vacate the judgment of conviction under C.P.L. 440.10. Our Court of Appeals has held that in order to preserve a challenge to the factual sufficiency of a plea allocution, a defendant must make either or both of those motions. *People v. Lopez, 71 N.Y.2d 662, 665 (1988).* Consequently, defendant's claims are entirely unpreserved and there is no reason for this Court to reach them in the interests of justice.

As a threshold matter, defendant's claim that his guilty plea was coerced is based, in large part, by allegations of misrepresentations made to him outside the record by counsel. In that regard, defendant claims that defense counsel advised him that if he pled guilty, the District Attorney would withdraw their death penalty notice. He further alleges that defense counsel advised him that he would face the death penalty if he went to trial. Finally, he asserts that defense counsel instructed him to answer all questions posed to him during the plea proceedings by stating "Yes, sir." Because of these misrepresentations, defendant now contends, the threat of the death penalty was planted in his mind and he felt he had no choice but to plead guilty and accept a sentence of life without parole, and he failed to advise the court of his feelings during the plea proceedings because of defense counsel's instructions that he only respond by stating "Yes, sir." Because these factual allegations are beyond the scope of the record, they must first be presented to the trial court in a motion to vacate judgment before they can be considered on direct appeal. *People v. Cooks, 67 N.Y.2d 100, 104.* Defendant having failed to present these contentions to the trial court in any form, they are not part of the record now before this Court.

Likewise, the remainder of defendant's claims are not preserved for appellate review because they were never presented to the trial court in the form of a motion to withdraw his guilty plea. *People v. Lopez, 71 N.Y.2d at 665.* In that regard, defendant now makes the following record-based claims: At no time was defendant advised that because he was mentally retarded, that he could not be sentenced to death; the District Attorney used the leverage of the death penalty to induce his guilty plea; the trial court never advised him that if he went to trial he could only receive life without parole and not the death penalty; defendant never stated he was waiving his right to a competency hearing to determine if he understood the proceedings; defendant's allocution failed to make out all the elements of the crimes of which he was convicted because it showed only that his codefendant was a merciless, manipulative killer who persuaded the defendant, his mentally retarded accomplice, to rob a restaurant where his codefendant worked as manager; defendant's guilty plea was contrary to *Hynes v. Tomei* because the threat of receiving the death penalty was left in defendant's mind, and he felt he had no choice but to plead guilty and accept life without parole. Because defendant failed to raise any of these claims before the trial court in a motion to withdraw his guilty plea, they are unpreserved for appellate review. *People v. Mower, 97 N.Y. 2d 239, 245-46 (2002).*

Analysis of preservation

This section is constructed on a spine of two procedural-bar contentions. Each one is separate and distinct from the other, and from the substantive argument refuting the merits of the defendant's claims. What is particularly noteworthy here is that each of the procedural bars would block not just one, but a large number of defendant's many claims.

RULE TWENTY

Your Legal Principles Must Be Stated Before Your Facts

Following your introduction, you have to explain to the reader the legal principles that apply to your issue before you attempt to persuade him or her that your facts compel the conclusion that you want the reader to come to. The legal principles involved will give meaning to your facts. If you are writing an exam answer, you'll be given the facts. But if you're writing a moot court brief, you'll be given materials from which you have to pull together a statement of facts. We'll explain how to write that narrative in Part Three. Right now, we'll focus on explaining the law.

EXAMPLE

Below is part of the law section from Linda Cantoni's reasonable doubt point in *People v. Bell* (see Rule Eighteen above):

> In *Victor v. Nebraska*, 511 U.S. 1 (1994), the United States Supreme Court held that "the Constitution neither prohibits trial courts from defining reasonable doubt nor requires them to do so as a matter of course." 511 U.S. at 5 (citation omitted). All that is required under the Constitution is that the court simply instruct the jury that the defendant's guilt must be proven beyond a reasonable doubt. *Id., citing Jackson v. Virginia*, 443 U.S. 307, 320, n. 14 (1979). Thus, "the Constitution does not require that any particular form of words be used in advising the jury of the government's burden of proof. Rather, 'taken as a whole, the instructions [must] correctly convey the concept of reasonable doubt to

> the jury.'" *Victor*, 511 U.S. at 5 (citations omitted). In *Jackson*, the Court explained that "[a] reasonable doubt, at a minimum, is one based upon 'reason.'" 443 U.S. at 317. Thus, jurors may not convict or acquit based upon some subjective whim. "A fanciful doubt is not a reasonable doubt." *Victor*, 511 U.S. at 17.

Analysis:

Notice how the paragraph clearly lays out the applicable legal principles: that the Constitution doesn't require a special reasonable doubt instruction; that the court simply has to tell the jury that they have to find the defendant guilty beyond a reasonable doubt; that a reviewing court will look at the instructions in their entirety to see if they were correct; and that a reasonable doubt is based on "reason," not a whim. No facts appear in this paragraph; it's not time for them yet. Sticking to the law at this point orients the judge to the principles that he or she is going to have to apply to the facts in order to make a decision, and that will, in turn, give *legal meaning* to those facts.

RULE TWENTY-ONE

Be Objective in Stating Your Legal Basis

The reader or judge must have confidence that you are fairly and accurately summarizing any applicable legal principles. To put it another way, if you fail to objectively summarize the applicable law, the reader will no longer have confidence in anything that you argue, even if the rest of your argument has merit. Remember, your ultimate goal is to persuade the reader that your argument is logical and fair. Persuasion is impossible without confidence, and in a legal argument, once you lose the confidence of the judge, you will have lost the argument. So above all else, when summarizing legal principles, you must be objective, accurate, and fair.

One of your most important classes will be your legal research course. There you will learn how to research case law, statutes and other materials. But having learned those techniques, you will then face the challenge of coping with law that often goes against your position. This won't happen, of course, on exams that require you to argue both sides of every issue. Once you begin to argue in moot court, however, your competitive juices will flow and you'll want to win. The surest way to lose, however, is to purposely misquote the law, by either ignoring relevant precedent or citing cases in a way that misrepresents the holdings of those decisions. All it takes is once—if you purposely misrepresent the law to your moot court judge on only a single occasion you will be viewed as someone who cannot be trusted. Don't do it. As a professional, your reputation will depend on the quality of your legal arguments. An argument built upon a false representation of the law is nothing less than a fraud.

RULE TWENTY-TWO

Use Block Quotes Sparingly

When you're writing a brief for moot court or a memorandum of law, you might be tempted to quote, line by line, from the cases or statutes that you believe support your position. A pithy, well-written quote certainly has its place. But more than a sentence or two will put a drag on your argument. Simply put, long, unwieldy block quotes on every other page are unreadable. They'll only interrupt the flow of your argument. You should, instead, merely summarize the law that you're relying on, in plain English. As long as you accurately summarize the law, there's no need for you to use block quotes. Your argument gains force if it flows, gathering momentum as the logic path becomes clear and irrefutable. When you block flow, you are shutting off persuasive power and breaking up the argument in your reader's mind. Every sentence of your argument should contribute to the argument's flow.

Exam questions, for the most part, seek to measure the breadth and depth of your understanding of the area of law tested as opposed to your mechanical memory of specific legal principles. Except in rare instances, the law is shaped by a line of decisions, as opposed to any single decision. There's a good reason for this: over time courts, especially the higher courts such as the United States Supreme Court, grapple with issues that have a profound impact on society as a whole. If the Court acts precipitously, its great power will be questioned, if not openly challenged. As matter of self-preservation, the Court, and most high appellate courts, move slowly and carefully, limiting the reach of each decision in order to avoid catastrophic resentment. When you are answering an exam hypo, show the grader that you've read and understood the applicable line of cases. You do that by explaining in plain English how that line of cases has developed, where the law currently stands, and even, for extra points, where you think it will go in the future. Merely quoting wholesale from a case or statute won't demonstrate your knowledge and understanding of the law. Just the opposite; and, in fact, it might even lead the reader to think that you're just lazy.

As we've said, a good quote does have its place. When a court has expressed something particularly well, or your argument depends in part on the wording of a decision or statute, quotes will help to demonstrate your point. But avoid the temptation to lay them on thick. Weed out the unnecessary parts of the quote by using paraphrasing and ellipses.

And while we're on the subject of things that bore the reader, a word about "string cites": Don't use them. No one likes to slog through citation after citation in order to get to your next sentence. If there are many cases or other authorities that support your position, pick the one or two most recent or most authoritative ones. When is a string cite appropriate? In rare instances, such as where an issue is a novel one in your jurisdiction, you may want to make the point that many courts in other jurisdictions have come down on your side of the issue. But that situation is indeed rare. In normal circumstances, keep the number of supporting citations to a minimum.

EXAMPLE

Take another look at the example used in Rule Twenty. It combines direct quotes from relevant case law with plain English sentences that paraphrase relevant language from the cases. Imagine how it would read if Ms. Cantoni had simply presented block quotes from the two United States Supreme Court cases cited, like this:

In *Victor v. Nebraska*, 511 U.S. 1, 5 (1994), the United States Supreme Court held:

> The beyond a reasonable doubt standard is a requirement of due process, but the Constitution neither prohibits trial courts from defining reasonable doubt nor requires them to do so as a matter of course. Cf. *Hopt* v. *Utah*, 120 U.S. 430, 440-441, 30 L. Ed. 708, 7 S. Ct. 614 (1887). Indeed, so long as the court instructs the jury on the necessity that the defendant's guilt be proved beyond a reasonable doubt, see *Jackson* v. *Virginia*, 443 U.S. 307, 320, n. 14, 61 L. Ed. 2d 560, 99 S. Ct. 2781 (1979), the Constitution does not require that any particular form of words be used in advising the jury of the government's burden of proof. Cf. *Taylor* v. *Kentucky*, 436 U.S. 478, 485-486, 56 L. Ed. 2d 468, 98 S. Ct. 1930 (1978). Rather, "taken as a whole, the instructions [must] correctly convey the concept of reasonable doubt to the jury." *Holland* v. *United States*, 348 U.S. 121, 140, 99 L. Ed. 150, 75 S. Ct. 127 (1954).

In *Jackson*, the Court explained:

> The *Winship* doctrine requires more than simply a trial ritual. A doctrine establishing so fundamental a substantive constitutional standard must also require that the factfinder will rationally apply that standard to the facts in evidence. A "reasonable doubt," at a minimum, is one based upon "reason." Yet a properly instructed jury may occasionally convict even when it can be said that no rational trier of fact could find guilt beyond a reasonable doubt, and the same may be said of a trial judge sitting as a jury. In a federal trial, such an occurrence has traditionally been deemed to require reversal of the conviction. *Glasser* v. *United States*, 315 U.S. 60, 80; *Bronston* v. *United States*, 409 U.S. 352. See also, *e. g., Curley* v. *United States*, 81 U. S. App. D. C. 389, 392-393, 160 F.2d 229, 232-233. Under *Winship*, which established proof beyond a reasonable doubt as an essential of Fourteenth Amendment due process, it follows that when such a conviction occurs in a state trial, it cannot constitutionally stand.

443 U.S. at 317 (footnotes omitted). Thus, jurors may not convict or acquit based upon some subjective whim. As the Court stated in *Victor*, 511 U.S. at 17:

> Finally, Sandoval objects to the portion of the charge in which the judge instructed the jury that a reasonable doubt is "not a mere possible doubt." The *Cage* instruction included an almost identical reference to "not a mere possible doubt," but we did not intimate that there was anything wrong with that part of the charge. See 498 U.S. at 40. That is because "'reasonable doubt,' at a minimum, is one based upon 'reason.'" *Jackson* v. *Virginia, supra*, at 317. A fanciful doubt is not a reasonable doubt. As Sandoval's defense attorney told the jury: "Anything can be possible . . . . [A] planet could be made out of blue cheese. But that's really not in the realm of what we're talking about." Sandoval App. 79 (excerpt from closing argument). That this is the sense in which the instruction uses "possible" is made clear from the final phrase of the sentence, which notes that everything "is open to some possible or imaginary doubt." We therefore reject Sandoval's challenge to this portion of the instruction as well.

Pretty dreadful, isn't it? The use of these endless block quotes, although they accurately state the law, forces the reader to wade through dense quoted language, much of which is irrelevant or unnecessary, and which is chock full of citations to cases that are not essential to the argument. The desired effect of the law paragraph—to lay before the judge a concise statement of the applicable law—is completely lost. Remember, a *point* is a set piece—you want the reader to be able to follow you along the path of your argument to its end without having to stop along the way to decipher any part of it.

Note also that it takes very little work to string together a bunch of quotes (or a bunch of cites) and let the reader figure it all out—and it shows. A critical reader—and in the law business, *every* reader is critical—will see at once that you didn't care enough to put any thought into your argument. It takes a lot more work to cull relevant, compelling quotes from lengthy passages in a decision, and to use them wisely as part of an argument of your own making. But that extra work is well worth it, because it not only makes the argument more effective, it also enhances your credibility immeasurably.

RULE TWENTY-THREE

Translate Legalese into Simple English

Not only must you avoid block quotes of legal text, you must also avoid turgid, overblown legalistic phrases. These stop the reader cold. The reader loses track of your argument, becomes irritated that he or she must struggle to understand what you are saying, and loses confidence in your overall ability to express your thoughts. The fact that you are relying on sound legal authority won't help you in the reader's eyes. In the real legal world, you have to assume that the judge wants your argument spoon-fed to her. No matter how intelligent the judge is, she wants her life made easy. She's got lots of cases to decide and lots of issues to deal with. The more difficult and complicated the concepts that you are trying to get across, the harder you should work to express them in simple, declarative sentences that can be gulped down like ice water on a blistering summer day. Keep in mind what we told you in Rule Three: The simple declarative sentence is your best weapon.

EXAMPLE

Justice Louis Brandeis, in his dissent in *Olmstead v. United States,* 277 U.S. 438 (1928), summed up his position in the following paragraph, constructed entirely of short, simple declarative sentences:

> Decency, security and liberty alike demand that government officials shall be subjected to the same rules of conduct that are commands to the citizens. In a government of laws, existence of the government will be imperiled if it fails to

> observe the law scrupulously. Our Government is the potent, the omnipresent teacher. For good or for ill, it teaches the whole people by its example. Crime is contagious. If the Government becomes a lawbreaker, it breeds contempt for the law; it invites every man to become a law unto himself; it invites anarchy. To declare that in the administration of the criminal law the end justifies the means—to declare that the Government may commit crimes in order to secure the conviction of a private criminal—would bring terrible retribution. Against that pernicious doctrine this Court should resolutely set it face.

This single paragraph, which in itself is a small masterwork, derives its power from its simple declarative sentences. When you read court decisions or legal texts, or letters and other documents drafted by lawyers, you will often find bombast made up of long, complicated sentences loaded with Latin references. Compare those poorly constructed passages to Brandeis' paragraph from *Olmstead* to remind yourself of the power of the short simple declarative sentence.

RULE TWENTY-FOUR

Conclude Your Law Paragraph with a Contention

You've boiled down any legal language that you're relying on to support your main argument. It's as easy to read and understand as the infomercials on the back of a cereal box. You still need a transition sentence that will nail down the law paragraph and set up the next part of your point, the application of the law to your specific facts. End with a bang, a statement that summarizes your position simply and clearly in light of the law you've just explained.

EXAMPLE

In the **Cahill** decision, the Majority reviewed the crime of burglary as part of its analysis related its review of the defendant's conviction for intentional felony murder. The defendant was convicted of a second count of first-degree murder based upon the theory that he killed his wife during the course of committing the crime of burglary. In constructing the argument for reversing that conviction, the Majority began by defining burglary as follows:

> Burglary is part of a larger category of criminal behavior that involves intrusion upon property (*Penal Law article 140*). The statutory hierarchy is relevant. The lowest degree of intrusion is criminal trespass (a violation), by which a person knowingly enters or remains unlawfully in or upon premises (*Penal Law § 140.05*). From there, a trespass becomes more serious, depending on the nature of the premises and whether the trespasser possesses certain weapons (*Penal Law § § 140.10, 140.15, 140.17*). The critical distinction between

> burglary and trespass is that a trespass in a building or dwelling is complete when a person knowingly enters or remains unlawfully in those premises. Burglary requires more. There can be no burglary unless the trespasser intends to commit a separate crime when entering or remaining unlawfully in a building (see *People v Gaines, 74 N.Y.2d 358, 547 N.Y.S.2d 620, 546 N.E.2d 913 [1989])*. Burglary is thus an aggravated form of criminal trespass, in which the aggravating factor is the trespasser's intent to commit a separate crime (see *People v Henderson, 41 N.Y.2d 233, 391 N.Y.S.2d 563, 359 N.E.2d 1357 [1976]*; see also CJI *Penal Law 140.25 (1)(b), at 1076, 1077)*.

In masterful fashion, Judge Rosenblatt ends his legal discussion of burglary and how it relates to first-degree murder with a simple sentence: "The case before us does not fit this statutory paradigm."

This sentence summarizes the Majority's position and provides a verbal bridge from the law paragraph to the section where the Majority applies the law to the facts of the case.

RULE TWENTY-FIVE

Link the Facts to Your Main Argument

The heart of your brief or memorandum of law is the section of the point that connects your unique facts to your main argument. Or, in a multi-point brief, it is the section of each point that connects your unique facts to the sub-argument of that point. Likewise, the crux of your answer to any exam hypo is the section that shows, from all sides, how the relevant law applies to the facts given to you in the hypo. In your own mind you can clearly see the linkage between your specific facts and your argument on any given point of your brief or issue on your exam. It's so obvious to you that you see no reason to express it. You assume that the judge is smart enough to make the logical connection by himself. Wrong. Don't assume anything.

Remember the teacher in grade school who insisted that you show your work when you solved a math problem? Back then you probably couldn't understand why just giving the right answer wasn't enough. But your teacher was right, because the same is true in argument. You must show the reader how you reach your conclusion.

The only way to do this is to patiently work out the logic for him through paragraphs that are constructed of contention topic sentences, followed by facts or legal principles that prove your contentions. On exam answers you will be showing the grader that you understand the issue from all sides.

How do you link up the facts and the law to your argument? Well, you don't accomplish this by merely restating facts that the judge has already read in your brief, or that were given to you in your exam hypo, and then stating a bald conclusion. This is the single most common error that law students and inexperienced lawyers make when they apply the law to the facts.

Instead, prove your contentions by showing the reader the legal significance of the particular facts of your situation. You do this by drawing inferences from those facts. Because certain events took place, then under the legal principles you have summarized, your conclusion is the only valid one. Your legal principles set yardsticks that are met if certain facts are shown to have occurred. Your contention topic sentence states that the legal yardstick has been satisfied by your specific facts. Then you prove that conclusion by showing, through inference, how your facts add up to a factual conclusion that satisfies the legal threshold. When you answer an exam hypo, you go through this process for all sides of any issue.

There are no shortcuts. Step by step, contention by contention, you must patiently stitch relevant facts to relevant legal principles, until the argument flows together like the seamless images that flash on the screen during a movie.

EXAMPLE

The *Cahill* **Chart** is your best reference for this rule. You'll see a box on both sides of the chart (the majority and the Graffeo dissent) for **factual contentions** that "prove" the **Main Argument**. These contentions show the legal significance of the particular facts of the case. In other words, the writer directs a spotlight at certain key facts, and once highlighted, draws an inference linking those facts to the **Main Argument**—the link here is that the highlighted facts ***prove*** the **Main Argument.**

The majority highlights the fact that Cahill procured cyanide long before anyone believed his wife could ever testify against him. From that fact, the majority draws a crucial inference: ***Because Cahill procured the poison before there was any indication that Jill could testify against him, his motive for procuring it was simply to kill her as opposed to having a desire to prevent her from testifying.***

The Graffeo dissent highlights the fact that although Cahill intercepted the cyanide in July, he didn't use it until three months later, only after his mother informed him that his wife was conscious and able to speak. From this fact the Graffeo dissent draws a crucial inference: ***If Cahill's only motive for killing his wife was rage, he wouldn't have waited three months to kill her. That he did so, acting only after he learned she could speak, supports the conclusion that he was moved to kill her to prevent her from talking to authorities and testifying at his upcoming assault trial.***

The ***Cahill*** decision is an invaluable study tool for you because the facts were, in large part, not disputed by either the majority or the dissent. They disagreed, vehemently, as to the inferences that could be drawn from those facts. As a result it can be said that man's life hung in the balance by a thread—the thread of inferences drawn by the majority from the facts. Had the dissent prevailed in convincing a majority of the court that its inferences were the only viable ones, James Cahill would be facing death by lethal injection.

RULE TWENTY-SIX

Legal References Should Be in Plain English

Just as you converted to plain English the legal principles you relied on in the law paragraph of your point, you must also boil down to simple English any legal principles that you refer to in the linkage paragraphs of your point. In other words, don't repeat the legal principles verbatim or try to make them more flowery this time around—you'll only bore your reader.

Remember, at this juncture you are linking up relevant facts to relevant legal principles in order to establish an "if-then" relationship between the two. This powerful logical connection must strike the reader like an arrow hitting the bulls-eye. That will only happen if your written expression of the connection is concise and clear.

EXAMPLE

The ***Cahill* Chart** shows that the majority, in the box titled "statement of applicable law," framed the legal test, in part, as follows: "A critical factor in assessing the weight of the evidence is whether defendant thought he could avoid an assault conviction by murdering his wife."

This concise statement of the law comes into play in the linkage section of the Majority opinion in the following paragraph:

> Beyond that, defendant had fully confessed to the assault and the prosecution had a powerful case without Jill's testimony. In confessing to the assault, defendant **admitted that he hit Jill on the head at least three or four times** with

> the baseball bat. He further admitted that he **struck her while she was unarmed**, thus foreclosing any plausible claim of self-defense. He also confessed to having **wounded himself**, a deception designed to make it look as if he acted in self-defense, and that he **attempted suicide** after the assault. ***In light of these candid disclosures, there is scant basis to believe that defendant thought he could avoid an assault conviction by murdering Jill.***

Notice how the majority makes the "if-then" connection by first listing the factual contentions that support the inference before connecting those facts to the law with the phrase "In light of these candid disclosures." The logic "arrow" hits the bulls-eye without any further discussion of the legal principle itself; rather, the legal principle becomes the tip of the arrow when connected to the factual contentions by a transition "if-then" phrase.

RULE TWENTY-SEVEN

Avoid the Straw Man

Another common error in making an argument in a brief is to attack your opponent's contentions before you've affirmatively proved your main argument. It might seem attractive to set up a straw man only to knock him down. But it's not very effective. All it does is call too much attention to your opponent's position, and not enough to yours.

If you've followed the format we've laid out for you so far, you've already avoided the straw man because your point now has an intro paragraph, a law paragraph, and a linkage paragraph that uses inferences to stitch together the relevant facts and law. In short, you've completed the affirmative section of your point. Now you can, if appropriate, address your antagonist's claims.

This structure will also guide you through your answer to an exam hypo. Your grader wants to see if you can spot the issues; do so by going through the facts and listing them. If you know the law, you will be able to "see" the legal issues raised by the facts. Then take the issues one at a time, using the format of intro to frame the issue, then law section to show the grader that you understand the relevant law, and then a linkage section applying the relevant law to the facts using contention topic sentences and proving those contentions by weaving together facts and law.

You've probably realized by now that in an exam answer, you don't have to repeat the law section when you present arguments for each side of any given issue. Your summary/analysis of the applicable law will apply to all sides of the issue. Your argument will change though when you apply that law to the facts. So, break down any long hypo into separate issues. Start your answer by framing the issue, delineating how it should be framed for each party. Then write your law section. And third, apply the relevant law to the facts for each side, showing the grader the alternative conclusions.

EXAMPLE

The ***Cahill* Chart** shows that both the majority and the Graffeo dissent delay attacking the other side's contentions until *after* they've written their intro, law, and linkage sections. Only then, after they've fully set forth their respective *affirmative* contentions, do they turn to attacking the opposition.

RULE TWENTY-EIGHT

Attack Your Opponent's Legal Principles

This rule and the two following apply to your moot court brief, or any brief or memorandum of law you draft for a litigation class or clinical law class where you have an opponent. First, look at your antagonist's legal principles. Chances are that he or she has misread or ignored a court decision or a statute, or cites law that does not apply to your situation. Or, he or she has misstated the applicable law. Or, he or she has ignored legal principles altogether, relying instead on a general sense of outrage and allegations of unfairness.

The best way to attack faulty legal principles is to correct them. By going beyond mere assertions that your opponent's version of the applicable law is wrong, and asserting once more the correct legal principles, you not only destroy the legal foundation for your opponent's conclusions, you also reinforce in the judge's mind your summary of the law.

Even if your opponent's legal contentions are correct, you can still point out that he has misapplied them to the facts of your case. In other words, you can distinguish the authorities he has cited, based on the facts and the inferences to be drawn from those facts.

RULE TWENTY-NINE

Attack Your Opponent's Facts

Your moot court problem will most likely come with a packet of materials including documents that will provide all parties with factual background. In a criminal case these might include police reports, lab reports, eyewitness accounts or a record of testimony taken in court. In a civil case you'll get depositions, medical reports, accident reports and eyewitness accounts. We'll discuss in the next section of the book how you put together a narrative statement of the facts. We'll assume for now that you and your opponent have written your respective versions of the facts.

In constructing your points of argument, you must also review your opponent's version of the facts, and the inferences that he or she draws from those facts. One or both prongs may be vulnerable. Your first line of attack will be the accuracy of your opponent's version of facts. Obviously, there may be a total disagreement between you as to the facts at issue in the dispute. Those are known as issues of credibility. In other words, who's telling the truth? Depending on the situation, you may be able to argue that the "testimony" or eyewitness accounts of your opponent's witnesses are incredible on their face. Or your materials may contain a decision by a trial or hearing court that held a fact-finding hearing to determine whose version is credible. You may want to challenge that court's findings of fact or you could make arguments as to why your witnesses are more credible than your opponent's.

Your second line of attack is more subtle. Even if your opponent accurately recites the facts underlying the dispute, he or she may draw completely different inferences from those facts. You must attack your opponent's inferences, showing how they are simply unsupported by the "record"—the materials provided to you.

EXAMPLE

Take another look at the ***Cahill* Chart**. You'll find no better example of the second line of attack referred to in this rule—attacking your opponent's factual inferences. As we noted above, the majority and the Graffeo dissent agreed as to the basic facts; but each vehemently contested the inferences the other side drew from those facts to support their opposing conclusions of law. For example, the majority felt that Cahill's mother's testimony about Jill having spoken to the nurses did not reveal what Cahill himself knew about Jill's condition and speaking ability, and thus did not prove that he was afraid that Jill would testify against him at the assault trial. The dissent, on the other hand, believed that the fact that Cahill never learned what his wife said to the nurses was irrelevant; what was significant was that she could communicate, and that Cahill was aware of that critical fact.

RULE THIRTY

Avoid the Defensive

Attack your opponent's account of the law, challenge his facts, distinguish his cases, turn his arguments to your advantage, or simply dispute them, but do not apologize. Whether you're writing a brief or making an oral argument, you must not allow yourself to be put on the defensive. Does that mean you should become offensive? Of course not. To some degree, you're always defending your position. The crucial distinction is one of tone. Even if you're on the defensive, you must avoid sounding like you're on the defensive. Your written points should have a tone that is as immediate as the actual sound of your voice. You must always take a positive tone, emphasizing the affirmative.

This is especially true in oral argument. In oral argument you must keep the structure of your written argument in mind. Your written contentions will enable you to defend your position in a positive manner by providing you with the points you want to make. If you're under attack during an oral argument, fall back on the proof that you've developed to support the contention under attack. You may find yourself repeating the same contentions over and over again, but that's unavoidable, particularly when the attacker continues to hit you with the same objections. Always maintain your poise and your positive tone. By positive we mean confident, without sounding arrogant or condescending. Always be firm but respectful, of both your opponent and the judge.

RULE THIRTY-ONE

End Your Point with a Conclusion Paragraph

Once you've finished attacking your opponent's contentions, you must return to the affirmative by concluding your point with a paragraph that mirrors your intro. This paragraph, like the intro, will once again restate your main and/or sub-arguments. You should re-summarize the major contentions that support them. Your final sentence should be your main or sub-argument, stated as an absolute conclusion supported by all that has come before it. If you have an alternative demand for relief, you can add it here.

EXAMPLE

Take a look at the concluding paragraphs of the majority opinion and Judge Graffeo's dissent in ***Cahill*** regarding their respective arguments on witness elimination murder:

> MAJORITY: "In weighing the conflicting inferences that can be drawn from the facts, **the proof leads us to conclude that defendant, to put it plainly, wanted to kill Jill at the hospital for reasons that had virtually nothing to do with her ability to testify against him.** The weight of the evidence does not support witness elimination as a substantial motive for the murder, and **we therefore hold that the conviction for murder in the first degree under Penal Law § 125.27(1)(a)(v) must be vacated.**"
>
> DISSENT: "In this case, **the jury could logically infer from all the evidence that defendant was driven by a desire to**

> **convince everyone, including his children, that Jill initiated the incident; that she attacked him with a knife; and that, in the course of protecting himself, defendant simply 'snapped.'** This is the story defendant told the police in April 1998 and this is the explanation that was ultimately presented to the jury. While this account would not avoid a criminal prosecution and might not engender jury leniency sufficient to produce an acquittal—and it did not in this case—defendant did succeed in preventing the jury from hearing the whole story. **With Jill's death, defendant knew that there would be no one left to directly dispute his version of the events on the night of the assault.** Defendant committed the ultimate act of domestic violence and, by killing the prime witness, he also impeded the truth-seeking function of a trial, which is precisely why witness elimination murder is among the crimes most strongly condemned in New York State. In my view, **if we faithfully apply the weight of the evidence standard of review in this case and give deference to the jury's unanimous finding, there is no basis to set aside defendant's conviction of witness elimination murder in the first degree** (see Penal Law § 125.27[1][a][v])."

Both of these concluding paragraphs demonstrate the effectiveness of restating the main contentions, both legal and factual, before ending with an affirmative, absolute statement of what the outcome ought to be.

RULE THIRTY-TWO

An Argument Is a Unified Entity

We've broken points down into components: intro, law, linkage section, attack section, conclusion. But each of your points should flow together, a unified set piece whose components merge together into a coherent seamless whole. The components will merge only if you bind your contentions and sub-contentions with neon-sign topic sentences and paragraph-ending sentences that set up the topic sentences of the next contention paragraph.

You've now completed all the rules related to presenting points of argument. As we stated at the outset, you will have to practice. Argument is a craft and you can only learn it by doing it. Re-read the examples in this book, dissect them, and then write your own practice arguments. You want to become a pro, a master at the game of argument. It's only by forcing yourself to construct your own arguments that you'll grow and develop as an advocate.

We'll show you in the next section how to think like a lawyer when it comes to presenting your facts. The law may be on your side, but you could still lose if you don't coherently narrate the relevant facts.

PART THREE: WRITING A STATEMENT OF FACTS

RULE ONE

Tell a Story

You probably associate "story" with a lie. This stems from childhood, when stories are told to us or when as children, we made up events and were chided for "telling tales." But the ability to write a compelling story is crucial in argument craft. The reader will want to know the factual basis for your claim, and you must be able to convey those facts in a way that emotionally involves the reader and prepares him for the contentions that you'll use to construct your argument.

Trial practice is beyond the scope of this book, but as a law student you should know from the outset that the belief that trial practice and appellate practice involve fundamentally different skills is false. Both trial practice and appellate practice are based on argument. A trial lawyer must be able to construct solid, persuasive arguments both on the facts and the law. For example, a trial lawyer will be required to present legal arguments as to why each and every item offered into evidence should be admitted over the other party's objection. And a trial lawyer's main argument to the jury attempts to persuade the jurors that one version of the evidence is the truth. A trial lawyer's arguments on the facts and the law will be based on the same structure you've learned in the first part of this book: contentions supported by legal principles or facts or both.

Trial lawyers may also have to present persuasive versions of the facts in writing. The quality of the memorandum of law submitted to the trial court may often determine the outcome of any appeal because the appellate lawyer may be limited to presenting only those arguments made below before the trial court (see Part II, Rule Nineteen, on procedural contentions).

The techniques that follow regarding our method of writing a factual narrative apply with equal force to telling a story to a jury or other fact finder in the form of an opening statement or summation. So, even if your goal is only to become a trial lawyer, keep this in mind: if it's not on the page, it's not on the stage.

EXAMPLE

The majority opinion in ***Cahill*** includes a concise but riveting narrative of the facts of the crime. Judge Rosenblatt *tells the story* of the crime, sparing no details of the brutal baseball-bat attack, the victim's injuries resulting from the attack, or the manner in which Cahill's wife died after Cahill poisoned her.

Using visual language, Judge Rosenblatt recounts the baseball-bat attack by focusing on the action:

> In early April 1998, defendant and his wife, Jill, signed a separation agreement but continued to live under the same roof at their home in Spafford, Onondaga County. On April 21, during a pre-dawn heated argument, defendant struck Jill repeatedly on the head with a baseball bat. The couple's two young children were nearby and Jill called out, urging them to call the police because their father was trying to kill her. After the attack, defendant phoned his parents for help. They soon arrived at the Cahill residence, along with defendant's brother and a family friend who was a physician. Having been summoned to the scene, the police found Jill lying on the kitchen floor. She was covered in blood, writhing in pain and moaning incoherently. Her left temple was indented from the injury.

Notice how each sentence of this paragraph furthers the action. From one action to the next, the reader follows the course of events with no digressions or comments by Judge Rosenblatt. As a result, he "shows" the reader what happened, as if the action were taking place on a television screen.

This is the essence of good story telling: *show* the action, *don't tell it.* Using this technique; Judge Rosenblatt "hooks" the reader into the action, emotionally involving her. You can't read the Majority's account of the baseball-bat attack without "seeing" the defendant swing the bat into his wife's head again and again, hear Jill Cahill cry out to her children to call the police, and then see Jill as the police found her, writhing in pain on the kitchen floor, moaning incoherently.

RULE TWO

Be Accurate and Objective

The reader will be persuaded by your recitation of the facts underlying your claim only if she believes that you've recounted them in an accurate and objective manner. Any misrepresentation of the facts, no matter how slight, will inevitably destroy your argument. The more objective you are in your account, the more reliable your version of events will be.

RULE THREE

Don't Editorialize the Facts

One of the oldest clichés is that there are two sides to every story. You can't escape this fundamental aspect of life. Your opponent is out to convince the judge that certain events took place, while you must present those events from a completely different point of view. Because you know how your opponent will want the judge to see things, you'll be tempted to argue over certain disputed facts or characterize specific events. Don't. You'll only weaken your narrative by interrupting its flow, and highlight your opponent's account of disputed incidents.

EXAMPLE

Although the majority and the Graffeo dissent in *Cahill* interpreted the facts in diametrically opposing fashion, Judge Rosenblatt in the majority's narrative of the facts, recounted in the example to Writing Rule One, avoids any mention of the dissent, focusing totally on the action. Had he digressed at that point to attack the dissent, he would have destroyed the flow of the narrative, ending the reader's emotional involvement in the account.

RULE FOUR

Banish the Word "Testify" From Your Account

If you write that your witness "testified" to certain facts, you might as well write that the witness lied. Your narrative will turn choppy and the judge will pause to reflect on the credibility of the individual witness. Just relate an event, citing to your source, whether it be testimony, a document, or a recording. The impact will be much more immediate, as you can see in these simple examples:

Distant: Mr. Jones testified that he saw Mr. Clemens throw a baseball through his window.

Immediate: Mr. Jones saw Mr. Clemens throw a baseball through his window.

But when you're describing the testimony of your opponent's witnesses, the "testify" technique works well to distance the witness from the facts, and make it look like he or she is only claiming that something happened.

EXAMPLE

Note how, in relating the facts in *Cahill* (see the example to Writing Rule One), Judge Rosenblatt makes no reference to "witnesses" or "testimony." He simply and effectively presents the action as though it were happening in front of the reader's eyes. Any reference to "testimony" or "witnesses" would have distanced the reader from the action.

RULE FIVE

Banish the Passive Voice

The next step is to make those events come alive on paper. To do so, you must use the active voice. Excise any passive verbs and replace them with active verbs to depict each event of your narrative spine.

Let's look at two ways to tell a story, one in the passive voice, one in the active voice:

Passive: The witch was pushed into the oven by Hansel and Gretel. She was baked into a giant gingerbread cake by the fire. Then she was eaten by the children.

Active: Hansel and Gretel pushed the witch into the oven. The fire baked her into a giant gingerbread cake. Then the children ate her.

Notice how the active voice is more compelling—and easier to read. It invites the reader to visualize what happened as if it were happening right now. By contrast, the passive voice slows the reader down. He or she has to wait until the end of the sentence to figure out who was doing what. The last thing you want to do is delay the reader when you're presenting your facts. Keep it clear and crisp by keeping your account as active and immediate as possible.

Sometimes, of course, the passive voice is appropriate, especially where who did what is unimportant or unknown. But you should use the passive voice seldom. Read through your facts after you've written them and see whether you've used the passive voice anywhere. Then start editing. Try to turn every passive phrase into an active one, where you can. You'll wind up with a much more effective statement of facts.

EXAMPLE

In ***Cahill***, Judge Rosenblatt uses the passive voice to describe transitional action by unknown "minor characters": "Defendant and victim were taken to different hospitals." Following this transitional bit of action, Judge Rosenblatt returns to the active voice in recounting Cahill's initial statements to the police: "After hospital personnel treated defendant for minor injuries, the police brought him to the stationhouse for questioning. At first, [Cahill] stated that Jill had instigated the argument and attacked him with a knife, causing some cuts and scratches on his body . . . ."

RULE SIX

Rely on Bare Facts

Let the bare facts convey your underlying message. Don't adorn the basic elements of your story with commentary or opinion. You will only weaken the effectiveness of your narrative. Editorializing breaks the flow of your narrative, making the reader aware that you're trying to manipulate him. Your narrative should have the clarity of spring water flowing over a rockbed. The reader should never become conscious of your guiding hand. Rather, he should be swept along by the momentum of the facts as your version of events moves to its conclusion.

EXAMPLE

Judge Rosenblatt's narrative of the baseball-bat attack in ***Cahill*** illustrates this rule. The bare facts convey the brutality of the assault far better than would be the case had the writer attempted to "characterize" the action by using adjectives to describe it. "Defendant struck Jill repeatedly on the head with a baseball bat" is much more effective than "He brutally beat her with a baseball bat." "Brutal" may mean different things to different people; but anyone can imagine the horror of being struck repeatedly in the head with a bat.

RULE SEVEN

Close the Gaps

Your narrative should be complete, but not overly detailed. Depict an event in concise sentences, leaving out irrelevant minor details. Concentrate on the behavior at the core of the event. All else is excess verbiage. Relate the spine of events, one at a time, describing conduct and conversations.

Don't leave out any relevant events, even if they hurt your position. Any substantial gap in your narrative will sidetrack the judge and cause her to wonder why you've left something out. She will no longer trust your rendition of the story, and you'll lose some, if not all, credibility. Once you have the spine of events down on paper, link them up with transition phrases.

EXAMPLE

In ***Cahill***, Judge Rosenblatt begins his narrative of the crime with the baseball-bat attack and ends it with the cyanide poisoning of Cahill's wife months later. Yet, the entire narrative consists of only five paragraphs. He accomplishes this by focusing only on the action at the core of each event leading up to the homicide, relating these events one after the other, often using only one action sentence for a single event. The result is a complete *story* of the crime with a beginning (the baseball-bat attack), a middle (Cahill's indictment for assault), and an end (Cahill's poisoning his wife).

RULE EIGHT

Don't Run from Inconsistencies

You can't avoid inconsistencies. Your argument will be destroyed if you fail to acknowledge inconsistencies or facts that hurt your case. Your opponent will hammer you with those very facts, and the judge will reject your version of events. Every case, no matter how strong, has its weaknesses and flaws. You must embrace them. By doing so, you'll deaden their sting. Your goal must be to make the judge trust your narrative of events as complete, reliable, and objective.

EXAMPLE

In a sense, Judge Rosenblatt's depiction of the crime in ***Cahill*** is at odds with the Majority's ultimate conclusion: Cahill's conviction of first-degree murder under the witness elimination theory was against the weight of the evidence. Yet, by fully rendering the crime in all its brutality, Judge Rosenblatt shifted the focus to the *law*—despite the brutality of the crime, the facts did not, in the majority's view, meet the legal test with respect to Cahill's motive for committing the crime. Had Judge Rosenblatt "softened" his account of the crime, the majority would have left itself open to attack on the ground that it failed to comprehend the violent nature of the Cahill's crime.

RULE NINE

Put Subheadings in Their Place

Subheadings are useful organizers, but don't become addicted to them. They should never be used in place of transition or introductory sentences. Even if you use them, your narrative of the facts should flow as if the subheadings weren't there. Like chapter breaks in a novel, your subheadings should reorient the reader's focus without disturbing the overall flow of the narrative. Keep them to a minimum, and use them only when your narrative is particularly complex. For example, you might use them when relating a lot of different events that occurred at different places at the same time, or, as suggested in the previous rule, to separate the underlying facts from the procedural events in the litigation.

Where you do use subheadings, make them meaningful but concise. A long subheading will interrupt the flow and annoy the reader. At the same time, a subheading that is too pat or general will give the reader no useful information.

RULE TEN

Dialogue Adds Realism

The events that make up the spine of your narrative will inevitably involve conversation between the participants. You can make those events come to life with quotations, but make sure that the quotes are short, and relevant to the issues in dispute. There is no point in quoting speech just for the sake of adding dialogue. If relevant, speech can be as much a form of conduct as physical action.

EXAMPLE

In a footnote in *Cahill*, the majority notes that a nursing assistant saw Cahill in the hospital, disguised as a janitor, about a week before the murder: "She noticed defendant because he 'looked like he had a wig on' and was not wearing the usual blue uniform of the hospital cleaning staff. When she saw defendant enter Jill's hospital room, she followed him in and asked if she could help him. He answered that he 'just came down to say hi to Jill' and left the room." These snippets of testimony and dialogue bring the events to life. One can almost see and hear Cahill, in his ill-chosen janitor costume, lying to the nursing assistant after being caught sneaking into Jill's room.

RULE ELEVEN

If You Have a Source, Cite It

As we noted in the first section of the book, your moot court problem will no doubt come with a packet of "exhibits". They may include various reports—medical, police, accident, or depositions or hearing/trial testimony from which you will be required to produce a statement of facts for your case. Just as you should cite to the sources of the legal principles you're relying on (see Part II, Rule Twenty), you should also cite to "the record"—testimony or documents—when you refer to their contents in your factual narrative.

RULE TWELVE

Complex Facts Require Simple Narratives

Your moot court "client's" dispute may involve multiple events stretching over a period of weeks or months or even years. No matter how complicated a history the dispute has, you must narrate that history in a simple, direct manner. The basic chronological narrative structure applies to both single—and multiple-event narratives.

EXAMPLE

In ***Cahill***, the majority opinion flows directly from its narrative of the crime into a narrative of legal proceedings that ensued as a result of Cahill's murder of his wife. The majority's brief recitation of the "facts" encompasses a period of time stretching from April, 1998 to January, 1999. Yet, because of the direct manner in which Judge Rosenblatt narrates the complex history, the reader has no difficulty following the course of events as if they occurred over a few hours rather than ten months.

RULE THIRTEEN

Name Names in Your Narrative

Don't be afraid to name names. The events of your narrative depict the behavior of people. Name those people. The first time that you refer to any person, use their full name, capitalize it, and print it in bold type. Thereafter, use only the person's last name, unless there are several people with the same last name. In that case, you will have to use first names or full names, unless you can identify them by titles such as "Mr." or "Ms." Some lawyers like to give their clients or "friendly" witnesses the benefit of a title like "Mr." or "Ms." or "Detective" or "Dr.," as appropriate, as a subtle mark of respect for the witness. If one of the witnesses is a child, you would of course use his or her first name in your narrative.

The exception to this rule is where you're referring to the opposing party. Referring to this person as "plaintiff" or "defendant," as appropriate, is a subtle psychological technique that serves, frankly, to "dehumanize" the other party. It makes your named client and your named witnesses seem more human to the reader.

EXAMPLE

Notice how both the majority and the Graffeo dissent in ***Cahill*** refer to the victim as "Jill" throughout their respective opinions. Obviously, they didn't refer to her as "Cahill" because the defendant had the same last name; but they both avoided depersonalizing her by calling her the "victim." Moreover, using her first name, rather than "Mrs. Cahill," was clearly an attempt to show sympathy for her.

RULE FOURTEEN

Your Narrative Should Be Riveting but Reliable

To anyone else, the subject matter of your moot-court "client's" dispute may seem unimportant. But it wouldn't be to a real client, and it shouldn't be to you. Your narrative of events should reflect your commitment to your client's cause—but without undue emotion. The narrative structure will channel emotion in a constructive direction and give it focus. When you depict the event or events that make up your client's dispute, make your account riveting. If you don't care, no one else will. On the other hand, if you engage in unfocused histrionics, your version of events will be rejected as mere ranting.

Adopt a tone that is objective. The facts themselves, if organized in a compelling narrative, will show the judge that you have a valid factual basis for your arguments. The judge must reach this conclusion on his own. If you browbeat him, it will only make him distrust your narrative. If you are objective in your presentation of the facts, the judge will trust your narrative. But trust can only come from within. You cannot impose it from without.

EXAMPLE

As we noted above, the majority opinion in ***Cahill*** could have downplayed the brutality of the crime in its narrative of the facts. But Judge Rosenblatt avoided that pitfall, choosing instead to let the facts speak for themselves. Even if you disagree with the majority's reversal of Cahill's first-degree murder conviction, you cannot fault Judge Rosenblatt's objective account of the crime, which pulls no punches in fully describing Cahill's criminal acts.

CONCLUSION

Think Like a Lawyer

When you pass the bar exam and become a full fledged attorney at law you will be undertaking a great responsibility. If you "practice law," you will be holding yourself out to other people as someone whose judgment and opinion can be relied upon. Often, people will entrust to you a key role in the most important decisions they will ever make. If you fail to protect them to the best of your ability, the consequences can be ruinous, to them and to you.

Even if you don't practice law, you will rely on your ability to analyze legal issues and construct clear, logical arguments. The craft of argument can be mastered. We hope this book has helped you to gain that mastery. Just as important, however, is that you practice this craft with a sense of honor and an awareness of the crucial role society has delegated to professional arguers, or attorneys. If you are guided by one principle through your career let it be this: don't misrepresent the law or the facts for your own personal gain or a client's gain.

We wish you a long and satisfying career, whatever path you choose.

And remember: Think Like a Lawyer!

APPENDIX

CAHILL CHART

Chart of Contentions in *People v. Cahill*

(Note: "FC" stands for "factual contention")

Majority Contentions (J. Rosenblatt)	Dissent Contentions (J. Graffeo)
Main Contention: Cahill's conviction for witness elimination murder was **against the weight of the evidence.** The evidence showed only that Cahill **poisoned his wife because she wanted to divorce him, not to eliminate her as a witness against him at trial on assault charges** stemming from his attacking her with a baseball bat.	**Main Contention: The jury properly weighed the evidence** and the conviction should be upheld. A substantial factor in Cahill's killing of his wife was his **desire to eliminate her as a witness at his upcoming trial for attacking her with a baseball bat.**
Statement of applicable law: The crime is proved if Cahill's motivation to eliminate his wife as a witness was a substantial factor in murdering her, even though he may have had mixed emotions. A critical factor in assessing the weight of the evidence is whether Cahill thought he could avoid an assault conviction by murdering his wife.	**Statement of applicable law:** The witness elimination statute is unconcerned with the probability of a conviction. The statute requires only proof that the murder was committed to prevent the intended victim's testimony.
Applying the law to the facts, the majority concludes that the verdict is against the weight of the evidence.	**Applying the law to the facts, the dissent concludes that there is no basis to set aside the jury's finding that Cahill was guilty of witness elimination murder.**
Primary Factual Contention That "Proves" Main Contention: The witness elimination theory is refuted by specific evidence.	**Primary Factual Contention that "Proves" Main Contention:** The jury properly weighed the evidence tending to prove witness elimination murder, and the majority is inappropriately substituting its own view of the evidence, based on a cold record, for that of the jurors who saw and heard the witnesses and sat in judgment on Cahill.

FC 1: Cahill procured cyanide long before there was any possible belief on anyone's part that Jill could ever testify at trial against him for hitting her in head with baseball bat.	**FC 1:** Cahill intentionally killed Jill to prevent her from challenging his version of "the truth" about the circumstances leading to his baseball attack on her (as opposed to preventing his conviction for assault).
FC 2: After the assault Jill was incapable of being a witness.	**FC 2:** Although the evidence showed Cahill intended to kill Jill when he attacked her with the bat, at the time of the assault and at trial he claimed Jill attacked him first and he initially responded in self-defense. This is the factual rendition of the assault that Cahill wanted the world to hear and believe.
FC 3: As late as August 1998, when Jill was in a coma rehabilitation unit, her cognitive abilities ranked at 5 or 6 on a 25-point scale.	**FC 3:** Jill survived the baseball bat attack and was beginning to communicate at the time of the murder.
FC 4: At Cahill's criminal proceedings on assault case, there was no mention that Jill might or possibly could testify against him.	**FC 4:** Once Cahill learned that Jill could speak, following his mother's visit to the hospital, he executed his plan to permanently prevent her from attempting to contradict his account of the truth.
FC 5: There was not a shred of evidence that Jill even retained a memory of the assault.	**FC 5:** Immediately after learning that he was to be indicted for assaulting Jill, and that his children were potential witnesses, Cahill began to search the Internet to buy cyanide.
FC 6: A prosecutor testified that up to the date of Jill's murder, no law enforcement official had even interviewed her about assault.	**FC 6:** Upon learning that his children would be subjected to psychiatric evaluations, Cahill had reason to believe his children would be questioned about the events surrounding the baseball bat attack.
FC 7: The brutality of the bat assault permits a "compelling inference" that even as of then, Cahill wanted to kill Jill, and that by poisoning her in the hospital, he fulfilled his previously formed intent, which sprang from the impending divorce.	**FC 7:** After Cahill's indictment on assault charges, and after he knew that the prosecution's plea offer required that he serve 10 years in prison, he decided to order cyanide on forged letterhead of a local manufacturing company. The next day Cahill rejected the plea offer in court.
FC 8: Cahill had fully confessed to assaulting Jill, and the prosecution had a powerful case without her testimony. Because of the confession, there was "scant basis" to believe that Cahill thought he could avoid the assault conviction by murdering Jill.	**FC 8:** Although Cahill intercepted the cyanide shipment in July, he didn't use it until three months later—only after he learned, from his mother, that Jill was conscious and able to speak.

	FC 9: During a visit to the hospital, Cahill's mother saw Jill speak to two nurses. She reported this to Cahill. This was the first time he learned that she could speak, and therefore posed a threat as a possible witness against him, and he immediately put his murderous plan into action.
	Main Argument restated: This sequence of events amounted to compelling evidence supporting the conclusion the jury unanimously reached: Cahill killed his wife to prevent her from communicating with authorities and testifying at the impending assault trial.
Attack on prosecution's contentions: The prosecution relied primarily on Cahill's mother's testimony, but her testimony does not reveal what Cahill knew about Jill's condition and speaking ability, and does not show that he was afraid that Jill would testify against him at the assault trial.	**Attack on majority's view of evidence: No other rationale accounts for Cahill's timing in carrying out his plan for murder. The majority bases its decision on facts that were not known to Cahill and therefore shed no light on his motivation. There was no evidence that Cahill was ever aware that Jill had never been interviewed by the police or prosecution, or that he knew whether she retained any memory of the assault. The fact that Cahill never learned what his wife said to the nurses is irrelevant; what is significant is that she could communicate and Cahill was aware of that critical fact.**
Supporting FC 1: Cahill's mother merely testified that Cahill told her, "I hope when this is all concluded that she can tell the truth about what led to the break-up of their marriage." This statement does not evince Cahill's fear of Jill's possible testimony in the assault trial; it is more a comment about the dissolution of his family.	**Supporting FC 1:** There was no other evidence presented to jury that explains why Cahill waited three months to kill his wife once he had the cyanide. There is no requirement in the statute that a defendant seek to avoid a **conviction**; only that a defendant seeks to prevent the intended victim's testimony.
Supporting FC 2: Cahill's mother testified that Jill "said something" to the nurses, and she told Cahill about Jill's physical condition. But we do not know what Jill said to the nurses or what Cahill's mother told him about Jill's status.	**Supporting FC 2:** The majority says that Cahill was motivated to poison his wife because their marriage and family life were being destroyed, not because he wanted to kill a witness in assault case. If that was the case, why did he not attempt to kill her **before** he learned that she had regained the ability to speak?

Supporting FC 3: Cahill's father stated that there wasn't a word spoken during the mother's visit to the hospital.	
Attack conclusion: Cahill's mother's testimony does not reveal what Cahill knew about Jill's condition and speaking ability, and thus does not prove that Cahill was afraid that Jill would testify against him at the assault trial.	**Attack conclusion:** In the absence of any plausible reason explaining why Cahill waited until mid-October to administer the cyanide, the jury was entitled to conclude that his motivation was to prevent his wife from communicating her version of the facts underlying the assault.
FACTUAL CONCLUSION: The proof leads to the conclusion that Cahill "wanted to kill Jill at the hospital for reasons that had virtually nothing to do with her ability to testify against him."	**FACTUAL CONCLUSION: The jury could reasonably infer that, whatever else may have led Cahill to take his wife's life, he intended to eliminate her as a witness.**
MAIN ARGUMENT RESTATED: The weight of the evidence does not support witness elimination as a substantial motive for the murder.	**MAIN ARGUMENT RESTATED: The jury could logically infer that Cahill was driven by a desire to convince everyone, including his children, that Jill initiated the assault by attacking him with a knife, and that in the course of protecting himself, he snapped. By killing Jill, Cahill succeeded in preventing the jury from hearing the whole story. With her death, Cahill knew there would be no one left to dispute his version of the events on the night of the assault. He committed the ultimate act of domestic violence and, by killing the prime witness, he also impeded the truth-seeking function of a trial.**

EXCERPTS FROM PEOPLE v. CAHILL, 2 N.Y.3d 14 (2003)

From the Majority Opinion by Judge Rosenblatt:

III. Guilt Phase

A. Defendant's Conviction Under *Penal Law § 125.27 [1][a][v]*

Witness elimination murder is committed when a defendant intentionally kills a victim who "was a witness to a crime committed on a prior occasion and the death was caused for the purpose of preventing the victim's testimony in any criminal action" (*Penal Law § 125.27 [1][a][v]* [emphasis added]). As a threshold matter, the parties dispute the thrust of the words "for the purpose of." Defendant argues that the crime is not made out unless a defendant kills the victim for the sole purpose of preventing the victim's testimony. He argues, in essence, that the verdict cannot stand if there was proof that he had any motive for the murder other than his desire to prevent Jill's testimony. The People contend that evidence of multiple motives may support a conviction for witness elimination murder.

Both parties cite the legislative memorandum, which states:

> "Killings must be committed 'for the purpose of' preventing, influencing or retaliating for prior testimony. Thus, this provision is applicable when there is both a defined victim characteristic, (witness, family member) and when it can be

> proven that the defendant's motivation for committing a killing was to prevent or influence the actual testimony of a victim in a criminal proceeding"

(Mem of Codes Comm, Bill Jacket, L 1995 ch 1, at 2). Like the statutory language, however, this recitation does not address mixed motives. We conclude that the statute would have to be read too expansively to authorize a conviction when a defendant's motivation to eliminate a witness is insubstantial or incidental. Conversely, we cannot imagine that the Legislature intended to exclude a defendant—whose motivation to eliminate a witness was a substantial reason for the murder—merely because the defendant may have had other reasons or motives for the murder. Accordingly, the statute is satisfied if defendant's motivation to eliminate Jill as a witness was a substantial factor in murdering her, even though he may have had mixed motives. Applying this standard, we address defendant's claim that his conviction for murder in the first degree based on witness elimination (see *Penal Law § 125.27 [1][a][v]*) is both legally insufficient and against the weight of the evidence. We conclude that the evidence adduced on this count is legally sufficient, but that the verdict is against the weight of the evidence.

CPL 470.30 directs that criminal appeals taken directly to our Court are governed by *CPL 470.15 and 470.20*, which in turn address the scope of our review and the corrective action to be taken upon reversal or modification. Pursuant to *CPL 470.15 (2) and (4)*, reversal or modification may be based on a determination that the evidence adduced at trial is not legally sufficient to establish the defendant's guilt. On the other hand, *CPL 470.15 (5)* allows for reversal or modification when a verdict is, in whole or in part, against the weight of the evidence.

Legal sufficiency review and weight of the evidence review involve different criteria. In assessing legal sufficiency, a court must "determine whether there is any valid line of reasoning and permissible inferences which could lead a rational person to the conclusion reached by the jury on the basis of the evidence at trial" (*People v Bleakley, 69 N.Y.2d 490, 495, 515 N.Y.S.2d 761,*

508 N.E.2d 672 [1987], quoting *Cohen v Hallmark Cards, 45 N.Y.2d 493, 499, 410 N.Y.S.2d 282, 382 N.E.2d 1145 [1978])*. By contrast, weight of the evidence review recognizes that "even if all the elements and necessary findings are supported by some credible evidence, the court must examine the evidence further" (*Bleakley, 69 N.Y.2d at 495*). An appellate court weighing the evidence "must, like the trier of fact below, 'weigh the relative probative force of conflicting testimony and the relative strength of conflicting inferences that may be drawn from the testimony'" (*id. at 495*, quoting *People ex rel. MacCracken v Miller, 291 N.Y. 55, 62, 50 N.E.2d 542 [1943])*. If "based on all the credible evidence a different finding would not have been unreasonable" and if the "trier of fact has failed to give the evidence the weight it should be accorded," the appellate court may set aside the verdict (id.). n23 When an appellate court performs weight of the evidence review, it sits, in effect, as a "thirteenth juror" (*Tibbs v Florida, 457 U.S. 31, 42, 72 L. Ed. 2d 652, 102 S. Ct. 2211 [1982])*.

n23 See also *People v Rayam (94 N.Y.2d 557, 560, 708 N.Y.S.2d 37, 729 N.E.2d 694 [2000])*; *People v Smith (63 N.Y.2d 41, 52, 479 N.Y.S.2d 706, 468 N.E.2d 879 [1984])*; *People v Davis (43 N.Y.2d 17, 36, 400 N.Y.S.2d 735, 371 N.E.2d 456 [1977])*; Karger, Powers of the New York Court of Appeals § 134(b), at 766 (3d ed).

Our dissenting colleagues are critical of our weight of the evidence analysis, claiming that this review is not an "open invitation" to substitute our own judgment for that of the jury. Of course that is true. But on the other hand, weight of the evidence review does not connote an invitation to abdicate our responsibility. A guilty verdict based on a legally sufficient case is not the end of our factual analysis but the beginning of our weight of the evidence review. Indeed, we are not only authorized to conduct this review but also constitutionally compelled to do so (*NY Const, art VI, §§ 3, 5*). Under the Constitution of our State, "in capital cases in which the sentence of death has been imposed, this court is vested with the power to and must review the facts" (*People v Davis, 43 N.Y.2d 17, 36, 400 N.Y.S.2d 735, 371 N.E.2d 456 [1977]*, quoting *NY Const, art VI, §§ 3, 5*; *People v Carbonaro, 21 N.Y.2d 271, 274, 287 N.Y.S.2d 385, 234 N.E.2d 433*). In *People v Crum (272 N.Y. 348, 6 N.E.2d 51 [1936])*, we underscored the importance of weight of the evidence review, noting that "we are obliged to weigh the evidence and form a conclusion as to the facts. It is not sufficient, as in most of the cases with us, to find evidence which presents a question of fact; it is necessary to go further before we can affirm a conviction and find that the evidence is of such weight and credibility as to convince us that the jury was justified in finding the defendant guilty beyond a reasonable doubt." (*id. at 350*). n24

> n24 This conclusion comports with the intention of the Framers of the 1894 Constitution: "The only thing, Mr. Chairman, I believe, which justifies making any exception to the proposed line of demarcation between [the Court of Appeals and the Appellate Division], one constituted to settle the law, and the other constituted to review the facts, is the sacredness of human life" (see Bergan, The History of the New York Court of Appeals, 1847-1932, at 215 [1985]).

Thus, because a death sentence appeal comes directly to our Court, we conduct this type of analysis, which is routine in Appellate Division review of criminal cases (*CPL 470.15 [5]*). There is nothing the least bit novel about Appellate Division weight of the evidence reversals. n25

> n25 Though far from commonplace, there are dozens of such instances(see e.g. *People v Gioeli, 288 A.D.2d 488, 733 N.Y.S.2d 242 [2d Dept 2001]*; *People v Scott, 283 A.D.2d 98, 728 N.Y.S.2d 474 [2d Dept 2001]*; *People v Vigliotti, 277 A.D.2d 890, 715 N.Y.S.2d 267 [4th Dept 2000]*; *People v McCoy, 266 A.D.2d 589, 699 N.Y.S.2d 131 [3d Dept 1999]*; *People v Alfaro, 260 A.D.2d 495, 688*

> *N.Y.S.2d 567 [2d Dept 1999]*; *People v Van Akin, 197 A.D.2d 845, 602 N.Y.S.2d 450 [4th Dept 1993]*; *People v Ruiz, 162 A.D.2d 350, 556 N.Y.S.2d 910 [1st Dept 1990]*). Of course, this is not a new phenomenon (see e.g. *People v. Beuther, 5 A.D.2d 1005, 173 N.Y.S.2d 680 [2d Dept 1958]*; *People v Moltesen, 282 A.D. 1090, 126 N.Y.S.2d 217 [3rd Dept 1953]*; *People v Smith, 234 A.D. 728, 251 N.Y.S. 999 [4th Dept 1931]*).

In arguing for witness elimination murder, the People drew upon certain events in defendant's life and matched them with steps he took toward planning Jill's murder. The People linked (1) the May 1998 Family Court appearances with defendant's Internet searches for cyanide; (2) the June and July 1998 developments in defendant's assault case with his procurement of cyanide; (3) defendant's October 1998 conversation with Patricia Cahill, defendant's mother, about her visit to Jill in the hospital with defendant's first disguised entrance into the hospital (in which a nursing assistant discovered defendant in Jill's room); and (4) defendant's upcoming Huntley hearing in the assault case with his having committed the murder. Viewed in the light most favorable to the People (see *People v Carr-El, 99 N.Y.2d 546, 547, 754 N.Y.S.2d 198, 784 N.E.2d 71 [2002])*, this timeline theory establishes a legally sufficient case. But it is barely that, and is decidedly against the weight of the evidence.

First, the May 1998 Family Court appearances primarily concerned the Cahill children. At the May 11 hearing, the Assistant District Attorney stated that the criminal court had issued an order of protection on behalf of the children and that they were potential witnesses in the assault case. The only evidence pertaining to the May 19 hearing involved psychological testing for the children. Jill's status as a witness was not mentioned during these hearings—in fact, Jill was not mentioned at all. The better part of the evidence reveals that defendant was motivated to poison his wife because their marriage and family life were being destroyed, not because he wanted to kill a witness to the assault case. n26

> n26 Judge Graffeo, in her dissent, states that "approximately one week later, defendant was present for another Family Court proceeding and learned that his children would undergo psychological evaluation. These impending interviews gave defendant reason to believe that his children would be questioned about the assault on their mother and the effect that it had on them. This had the potential to elicit additional information regarding the events surrounding the assault" (dissent at 21). The only record evidence concerning this court date is a one-page "Family Offense Record of Proceeding." It notes the appearance of defendant, his counsel, Jill's attorney, the children's law guardian and Jill's parents. It further notes that the purpose of the hearing is an "original application" and that the status of the hearing was adjourned to June 18, 1998. A handwritten note states "Dr. Gordon to take psych/test of children (per LG) to set up schedule." The dissent's contention about the nature of the questioning is speculative. Nothing in this court record indicates that the children's psychological evaluation had anything to do with the criminal case. Rather, they were being evaluated by a psychologist in connection with the Family Court proceeding.

Using the prosecution's timeline, a critical feature refutes its witness elimination theory: defendant procured potassium cyanide long before there was any possible belief—on anyone's part—that Jill could ever testify at a trial, given her condition. n27 After the assault, Jill suffered from a host of medical complications that utterly incapacitated her as a witness. Further, one doctor testified that as late as August 1998, when Jill entered the coma rehabilitation unit, her cognitive abilities ranked at a five or six on a 25-point scale. Moreover, at the corresponding criminal proceedings, there was no mention that Jill might or possibly could testify against defendant. Indeed, there is not a shred of evidence in this record that Jill had even retained a memory of the assault.

Most compellingly, an Assistant District Attorney testified that up to the date of Jill's murder no law enforcement official had even interviewed her about the assault.

> n27 Judge Graffeo states that "the timing of pertinent events—when defendant actually ordered the cyanide, when he obtained it, and when he used the poison—forcefully demonstrates that defendant's actions were inextricably related to the prosecution of the assault charges" (dissent at 21). The dissent then mentions that between the date of defendant's arraignment on the assault indictment, and his next court appearance, there were numerous conversations between the People and the defense about the assault case. The dissent ignores that defendant first searched the Internet for cyanide information on May 11, 1998, only three weeks after the assault and one month before he was arraigned on the indictment on June 16, 1998.

In seeking to prove that defendant knew Jill was able to speak and was afraid of what she would say, the People relied largely on the testimony of Patricia Cahill, defendant's mother. She merely testified, however, that defendant told her that "I hope when this is all concluded that she can tell the truth about what led to the break-up of their marriage." This statement does not evince defendant's fear of Jill's possible testimony in the assault trial; it is more a comment about the dissolution of his family. In addition, Patricia Cahill testified that, during a visit, Jill "said something" to the nurses, and also that she told defendant about Jill's physical condition. But we do not know what Jill said, or what Patricia Cahill told defendant about Jill's status. Furthermore, Fred Russell, Jill's father, stated that "there was not a word spoken" during Patricia Cahill's visit to the hospital. Thus, Patricia Cahill's testimony does not even suggest, let alone reveal, what defendant knew about Jill's condition and speaking ability. It does not begin to show that he was afraid that Jill would testify against him at the assault trial. n28

> n28 Defendant also argues that the People improperly attempted to impeach Patricia Cahill, their own witness. *CPL 60.25 (1)* states that when the testimony of a party's witness on a material issue tends to disprove the party's position, the party can introduce a contradictory previous written statement signed by the witness or an oral statement given under oath. Defendant objected to the prosecutor's improper attempts at impeachment and the trial court sustained the objections. Thus there is no cognizable error.

Additional factors rebut the witness elimination theory. The very brutality of the April 1998 assault permits the compelling inference that, even as of then, defendant wanted to kill his wife and that ultimately doing so fulfilled his previously formed intent, which sprang from the impending divorce. n29

> n29 Judge Graffeo states that "if it was only hatred and family disruption that impelled defendant's murderous intent, why didn't he attempt to kill Jill in August after his parents surrendered custody of the children to Jill's parents, further removing him from his children?" However, defendant's parents did not lose all contact with their grandchildren. Rather, an August 20 transcript shows that by stipulation, all of the grandparents agreed that Jill's parents would take temporary custody of the children and defendant's parents would have alternate weekend visitation, as well as one school night per week.

Beyond that, defendant had fully confessed to the assault and the prosecution had a powerful case without Jill's testimony. In confessing to the assault, defendant admitted that he hit Jill on the head at least three or four times with the baseball bat. He further admitted that he struck her while she was unarmed, thus foreclosing any plausible claim of self-defense. He also confessed to having wounded himself, a deception designed to make it look as if he acted in self-defense, and that he attempted suicide after the assault. In light of these candid disclosures, there is scant basis to believe that defendant thought he could avoid an assault conviction by murdering Jill.

In weighing the conflicting inferences that can be drawn from the facts, the proof leads us to conclude that defendant, to put it plainly, wanted to kill Jill at the hospital for reasons that had virtually nothing to do with her ability to testify against him. The weight of the evidence does not support witness elimination as a substantial motive for the murder, and we therefore hold that the conviction for murder in the first degree under *Penal Law § 125.27 (1)(a)(v)* must be vacated.

Dissenting opinion by Judge Graffeo:

II. *Penal Law § 125.27(1)(a)(v)*: Witness Elimination Murder

The majority sets aside defendant's conviction of witness elimination murder because it believes that the jurors, who had the opportunity to see and hear the witnesses and assess their credibility, failed to properly evaluate the evidence presented at trial. In doing so, the majority substitutes its view of the evidence, based on the cold record, for that of the jurors who sat in judgment of defendant. Because I cannot agree that the jury failed to properly weigh the evidence in this domestic violence case, I would uphold defendant's conviction under *Penal Law § 125.27(1)(a)(v).*

According to the majority, a critical factor in assessing the weight of the evidence in this case is whether "defendant thought he could avoid an assault conviction by murdering Jill" (maj op at 45-46). The witness elimination statute, however, is unconcerned with the probability of a conviction. The plain language of the statute requires only proof that the murder was committed to "prevent[] the intended victim's testimony" (*Penal Law § 125.27[1][a][v]*).

> n6 Our task is to determine whether the jury's assessment of this statutory requirement was against the weight of the

> evidence. n6 The relevant statutory text reads: "[a] person is guilty of murder in the first degree when * * * with intent to cause the death of another person, he causes the death of such person or of a third person; and * * * the intended victim was a witness to a crime committed on a prior occasion and the death was caused for the purpose of preventing the intended victim's testimony in any criminal action or proceeding."

People v Bleakley (69 N.Y.2d 490, 515 N.Y.S.2d 761, 508 N.E.2d 672 [1987]) provides the standard for weight of the evidence review:

"If based on all the credible evidence a different finding would not have been unreasonable, then the appellate court must, like the trier of fact below, 'weigh the relative probative force of conflicting testimony and the relative strength of conflicting inferences that may be drawn from the testimony' * * *. If it appears that the trier of fact has failed to give the evidence the weight it should be accorded, then the appellate court may set aside the verdict" (*id. at 495*).

This is not an open invitation for a court to substitute its judgment for that of the jury. Bleakley commands that "great deference" be accorded to the jury's resolution of factual issues (id.), a principle the majority fails to even mention. Deference is an integral ingredient of the weight of the evidence analysis because it is the "fact-finder[]" that has the "opportunity to view the witnesses, hear the testimony and observe demeanor" (*id.*)

Thus, although an appellate court engaging in weight of the evidence review has been described as fulfilling the role of a "thirteenth juror" (see *Tibbs v Florida, 457 U.S. 31, 42, 72 L. Ed. 2d 652, 102 S. Ct. 2211 [1982]*; *People v Rayam, 94 N.Y.2d 557, 560, 708 N.Y.S.2d 37, 729 N.E.2d 694 [2000])*, this shorthand is not a literal description of the court's appropriate analytical process. To the contrary, there are "without question * * * differences between what the jury does and what the appellate court does in weighing evidence" (*People v Bleakley, 69 N.Y.2d at 495*), which is apparent given that a jury's ability to assess credibility and weigh competing inferences is far superior to that of an appellate court working with only a "printed record" (*People v Cohen, 223 N.Y. 406, 423, 36 N.Y. Cr. 419, 119 N.E. 886 [1918]).* Jurors use all of their senses to evaluate testimony and evidence presented at trial—only they "are able and entitled to assess, at first hand, the credibility and reliability of the witnesses" because they have the opportunity to actually see, hear and feel the evidence in person (*People v De Tore, 34 N.Y.2d 199, 206, 356 N.Y.S.2d 598, 313 N.E.2d 61 [1974]).* A healthy respect for the jury's unanimous assessment of the evidence is therefore a necessary component of a proper weight of the evidence review.

Applying the Bleakley standard in its entirety, I cannot concur with the majority's conclusion that the jury verdict on the witness elimination count was against the weight of the evidence. The People presented compelling evidence that defendant intentionally killed his wife to prevent her from challenging his version of "the truth" about the circumstances leading to the assault on April 21, 1998. As the majority recognizes, the evidence overwhelmingly established that defendant intended to kill Jill when he assaulted her with a baseball bat, crushing her skull. But defendant offered a different explanation at the time of the assault and at trial, claiming that Jill attacked him first and he initially responded in self-defense. n7 This is the factual rendition of the assault that defendant wanted the world to hear and believe.

n7 Defendant initially gave the following statement to the police: "Around 4 or 4:15 AM this morning April 21, 1998 I was awakened by Jill. She grabbed my face and wrenched me over and then grabbed my arms and held me down. She was saying words to the effect, I'm not going to live here * * * indicating she no longer had a life here. I then got up and went downstairs. She followed me down and was yelling at me. * * * I had went in the kitchen and was standing near the refrigerator. Jill came into the kitchen. The argument continued, Jill went to the opposite side of the room * * *. Jill picked up a knife * * * sort of like a filllet [sic] knife with

> maybe a 6 to 7 inch tapered blade. * * * I tried to take the knife from her. She struck at me cutting my left forearm. I got a hold of her, in a position with her facing away from me with my arms around her and forced her out the back door of the house into a mud room. I [sic] As we were going out she was calling to the children, call the police, your father is trying to kill me. I pushed her to the floor and we wrestled a bit. She continued to call to the children. I pushed up and turned to get away, she was on the floor face down. I saw several baseball bats hanging on the wall and grabbed one. I turned to face her again and she was getting up facing me with her hands about chest high. She still had the knife in her right hand. I swung with the bat hitting her on the left side of the head. As I swung she raised her hands alongside her head. She started to move backwards and I swung again. This time she went backwards falling out of the back door onto a concrete patio * * *."
>
> In his later statement, however, defendant stated: "after she pulled the knife * * * I got Jill in a bear hug type position with her back to me. I got Jill out to the mud room and down on the floor. I got up got the baseball bat and Jill was on her feet with the knife in her right hand I swung the bat twice at her and on the second swing, I hit Jill on the head. Jill fell back and out the door * * *."

Yet, Jill Cahill survived the first attack. Over the next six months, she fought back from the brink of death to the point that she was able to respond and speak. The testimony of medical personnel and her family members clearly relayed to the jury that Jill was beginning to communicate in October 1998. What would she have testified to had she been given the chance—that she did not attack defendant with a knife and initiate the assault? We will never know. But we do know that, once defendant learned Jill could speak—after his mother visited Jill in the hospital in October 1998—he immediately executed his plan to permanently prevent her from attempting to contradict his account of "the truth."

In overturning the jury verdict on this count, the majority overlooks a number of significant facts and fails to identify the important connections between them that the jury may have found determinative. During the May 11, 1998 Family Court hearing, an Assistant District Attorney announced the People's intention to indict defendant for the April assault and advised defendant that his children were potential witnesses. The same day, defendant began to search the internet for websites relating to "cyanide." Approximately one week later, defendant was present for another Family Court proceeding and learned that his children would undergo psychological evaluation. These impending interviews gave defendant reason to believe that his children would be questioned about the assault on their mother and the effect that it had on them. This had the potential to elicit additional information regarding the events surrounding the assault. After the Family Court appearance, defendant returned home and searched the internet for information on "ordering potassium cyanide."

The timing of pertinent events—when defendant actually ordered the cyanide, when he obtained it, and when he used the poison—forcefully establishes that defendant's actions were inextricably related to the prosecution of the assault charges. Between the date defendant was arraigned on an indictment charging him with three counts of first-degree assault and his next court appearance, defense counsel and the prosecutor had "numerous conversations" about the case, including plea negotiations. Defendant's decision to order cyanide on the forged letterhead of a local manufacturing company on July 8 occurred only a day before the People's plea offer was officially placed on the record. The offer, under which defendant would have had to serve at least ten years in prison, was not accepted by defendant, making a trial increasingly certain.

Most importantly, although defendant intercepted the shipment of cyanide on July 17 by approaching the delivery person and taking possession of the package from the supplier he had contacted, he did not use the poison to kill his wife until three months later. Why? The evidence presented to the jury pointed to a logical explanation: defendant did not execute his homicidal plan until he was able to confirm that Jill was conscious and had recovered sufficiently to be a "threat."

Defendant's mother supplied defendant (and the jury) with the information that provided the impetus for him to carry out Jill's murder. n8 During a visit with Jill Cahill in the hospital on October 5, Mrs. Cahill observed a "conversation" between Jill and two nurses. Significantly, Jill actually spoke to the nurses. Defendant's mother told her son about these "physical observations" of Jill about two weeks later. Defendant's response to his mother demonstrates that he appreciated the significance of this information and knew that Jill was regaining her ability to communicate: "I hope when this is all concluded that she can tell the truth about what led to the break-up of the[] marriage." For the first time since the April assault, defendant became aware that Jill could speak and, therefore, posed a threat as a possible witness against him at trial. Defendant immediately put his murderous plan into action.

n8 The record does not suggest that defendant's mother intended to assist her son and she was never charged with any crime.

Within days of learning of Jill's improved condition and ability to speak, defendant—disguised as a janitor—was found in Jill's hospital room by a nurse's assistant. He quickly departed without incident but returned one week later, again in disguise. This time he was able to bring his plan to fruition—he murdered Jill by poisoning her with cyanide. Defendant had successfully eliminated the primary witness to the April baseball bat attack. n9 A hearing to determine whether defendant's confessions could be used at the assault trial was only days away.

n9 According to defendant's confessions, his children saw defendant beat their mother in the head with the baseball bat and heard her pleas for help. At one point, Jill called out

> to her daughter, begging her "to call the police, your father is trying to kill me." However, nothing in the record suggests that the children witnessed (or defendant believed that they had witnessed) what transpired between defendant and Jill before he began attacking her with the bat.

Giving due deference to the jurors' assessment of the evidence presented, this sequence of events amounted to compelling evidence supporting the conclusion the jury unanimously reached—defendant killed Jill Cahill to prevent her from communicating with the authorities and testifying at the impending assault trial. The trigger for the murder was defendant's awareness of the fact that Jill had regained her ability to speak, and with that ability, Jill may have refuted defendant's account of the events on the night of the assault.

Indeed, no other rationale accounts for defendant's timing in carrying out his plan for murder. The majority posits that defendant was motivated "to poison his wife because their marriage and family life were being destroyed, not because he wanted to kill a witness to the assault case" (maj op at 42). Defendant may have been motivated to kill because of the deterioration of his family life but the proof does not support the conclusion that this was his only motivation. And what other evidence was presented to the jury to explain why defendant waited three months after he acquired cyanide to carry out his plan to poison Jill? If it was only hatred and family disruption that impelled defendant's murderous intent, why didn't he attempt to kill Jill in August after his parents surrendered custody of the children to Jill's parents, further removing him from his children? In the absence of any plausible reason explaining why defendant waited until mid October to attempt to administer the cyanide—notably, just a day or two after his mother informed him of Jill's improved condition and shortly before the pretrial Huntley hearing scheduled for November 2—the jury was entitled to conclude that defendant's motivation was to prevent Jill from communicating her version of the facts underlying the assault. Hence, the jury could reasonably infer that, whatever else may have driven defendant to take Jill's life, he intended to eliminate Jill as a witness. Therefore, giving "great deference" to the jury's findings (*People v Bleakley, 69 N.Y.2d at 495*), I conclude that defendant's conviction of witness elimination murder was not against the weight of the evidence.

The majority's reasons for disregarding the jury's resolution of these issues focus on facts that were not known to defendant and therefore shed no light on his motivation. For example, there is no basis in the record to suppose that defendant was aware about the fact the majority finds "most compelling[]"—that Jill had never been interviewed by the police or a prosecutor (maj op at 43-44)—nor was there any proof that defendant knew whether Jill had or had not retained her memory of the events surrounding the assault (maj op at 43). These facts are meaningless to the witness elimination analysis because defendant's motives for acting could not have been influenced by that which he did not know. What is pertinent is that the jury heard evidence permitting the inference that defendant believed Jill posed a risk and he killed her to prevent her from testifying.

Similarly unavailing is the majority's decision to discount the importance of the evidence provided by defendant's mother. The majority claims that her "testimony does not even suggest, let alone reveal, what defendant knew about Jill's condition and speaking ability" (maj op at 44). That assertion is not borne out in the record. Defendant's mother testified that she told defendant about her observations of Jill's physical condition. This testimony came moments after she described to the jury what she had observed—that Jill spoke to the nurses. It is irrelevant that "we do not know what Jill said" (maj op at 44)—what is significant is that Jill could communicate and defendant was aware of this critical fact.

The majority also places undue emphasis on its conclusion that "there is scant basis to believe that defendant thought he could avoid an assault conviction by murdering Jill" (maj op at 45). The witness elimination statute does not require proof that defendant intended to avoid a criminal conviction. Rather, the statute requires only that a defendant seeks to "prevent[] the intended victim's testimony" (*Penal Law § 125.27[1][a][v]*). The facts of this case highlight the difference between the plain language of the statute and the majority's interpretation. It is true that defendant admitted that he beat Jill with a baseball bat during the April assault, although this was not a full confession since defendant maintained he did so in self-defense. The prosecution clearly had a "powerful case without Jill's testimony" (maj op at 45)—defendant confessed to wounding himself and acknowledged striking Jill after she had been incapacitated, thereby severely undermining if not "foreclosing any plausible claim of self-defense" (maj op at 45). But in order to convict defendant of witness elimination murder, the jury was not required to find that defendant hoped (either reasonably or unreasonably) that by killing Jill he could avoid a criminal prosecution. The jury had only to conclude that defendant intended to prevent her testimony.

In this case, the jury could logically infer from all the evidence that defendant was driven by a desire to convince everyone, including his children, that Jill initiated the incident; that she attacked him with a knife; and that, in the course of protecting himself, defendant simply "snapped." This is the story defendant told the police in April 1998 and this is the explanation that was ultimately presented to the jury. While this account would not avoid a criminal prosecution and might not engender jury leniency sufficient to produce an acquittal—and it did not in this case—defendant did succeed in preventing the jury from hearing the whole story. With Jill's death, defendant knew that there would be no one left to directly dispute his version of the events on the night of the assault. Defendant committed the ultimate act of domestic violence and, by killing the prime witness, he also impeded the truth-seeking function of a trial, which is precisely why witness elimination murder is among the crimes most strongly condemned in New York State. In my view, if we faithfully apply the weight of the evidence standard of review in this case and give deference to the jury's unanimous finding, there is no basis to set aside defendant's conviction of witness elimination murder in the first degree (see *Penal Law § 125.27[1][a][v]*).

III. Conclusion

The extreme disagreement that envelops the members of this Court stems from three general ideas and differing philosophies about how we should exercise the power that the State Constitution vests in this institution. By failing to respect the plain language of the first-degree felony-murder provision, the majority has substituted its "wisdom" and public policy choices for those of the Legislature when it enacted the statute. The majority also rejects the jury's assessment of the probative value of the evidence and the reasonable inferences derived therefrom. Finally, the majority sets aside the conclusions reached by the trial judge, who had the ability to actually see and hear the prospective jurors discuss their ability to fairly consider possible sentences, reinterpreting the statements made during the life and death qualification process from the cold record. In this case, I would respect, rather than second guess, the life/death qualification assessments of the trial judge, the factual findings of the jury and the public policy choice made by the Legislature.